It Wasn't for Nothing

A Powerful Story of Faith

Michaele Aldophe

ISBN

Hardcover: 979-8-9991010-0-6

Paperback: 979-8-9991010-1-3

Acknowledgments

Dear God,

Thank You for always being by my side, especially in the moments when I have felt lost, broken, or alone. There have been times when my heart has been heavy, and my spirit has been weary, but in those moments, You have wrapped Your arms around me, reminding me that I am never truly alone. Your love is a refuge, a place where I find comfort, peace, and the strength to keep moving forward.

Lord, I am deeply grateful for Your presence in my life. No matter how hard the journey gets, no matter how many obstacles stand in my way, You always remind me that You are with me. When I am overwhelmed by fear or uncertainty, You whisper words of reassurance into my soul. When I feel like giving up, You strengthen my heart and help me stand again.

There have been days when I didn't know how I would make it through when the weight of life's struggles felt too much to bear. But in those moments, You have carried me. When I cried out in pain, You heard me. When I felt unworthy, You reminded me that I am loved. When I was weak, You became my strength. Your faithfulness is unwavering, and Your love is unchanging.

Lord, I thank You for the quiet moments when You remind me to breathe, to be still, and to trust in You. In the chaos of life, You are my peace. In the storms, You are my anchor. In my joys, You are my source of all goodness. You have shown me time and time again that Your plans for me are good, even when I do not understand them.

I surrender my worries, my fears, and my doubts to You. I trust that whatever lies ahead, You will guide me, protect me, and lead me to where I am meant to be. I may not always see the bigger picture, but I know that You are working all things together for my good.

Thank You, Father, for loving me so deeply, for holding me so tightly, and for reminding me that no matter what happens, I am never alone. You are my refuge, my strength, my hope, and my greatest blessing.

In Jesus' name, I pray.

Amen.

Dear Mom and Dad,

Thank you for paving the way for me. Every sacrifice you made, every challenge you overcame, and every lesson you taught has shaped me into the person I am today.

You have shown me what it means to work hard, to persevere, and to never give up, no matter how difficult the journey may be. Because of you, I understand the value of dedication and resilience. Your sacrifices did not go unnoticed, and I carry them with me in everything I do.

I will always cherish the lessons you have taught me and will do my best to make you proud.

With all my love and gratitude,

Michaele.

Dear Matthew,

I am so lucky to call you my son. From the moment you came into my life, you have been a source of endless joy, love, and pride. Watching you grow into the amazing person you are today fills my heart with gratitude and happiness.

You are such a beautiful kid—not just on the outside, but in the kindness you show, the love you give, and the way you brighten the lives of everyone around you. Your smile, your laughter, and your spirit bring so much warmth to my heart.

Every day, I am in awe of your strength, your curiosity, and your ability to see the good in the world. You have such a kind and loving heart, and I know that wherever life takes you, you will continue to shine. Never forget how special you are and how deeply you are loved.

I am so proud of you, Matthew. No matter what, I will always be here for you, cheering you on, supporting you, and loving you with all my heart.

With all my love,

Mom.

Dear Self,

Gosh, I am so proud of you. I know how much you've been through and how many challenges you've faced, and yet, here you are—standing strong, pushing forward, and becoming the person you were always meant to be. You have come so far, and I want you to take a moment to recognize just how incredible that is.

There were times when you doubted yourself, moments when you questioned whether you could keep going. But look at you now. You didn't give up. You found the strength within you to rise above the obstacles, to keep moving even when the path was uncertain. That strength, that resilience, is something to be proud of.

You have grown in ways you never thought possible. You've learned to love yourself, to embrace your flaws, and to celebrate your victories—big or small. You have become someone who is worthy of all the love, success, and happiness that is coming your way.

No matter what lies ahead, never forget how far you've come. Keep believing in yourself, keep pushing forward, and keep embracing the journey. You are capable, you are strong, and you are worthy of everything you dream of.

With love and pride,

Me.

Introduction

Every journey has a purpose, even when it's hard to see at first. My story isn't just about me—it's about faith, resilience, and the unwavering love of a mother for her child. It's about believing in miracles, even when the world says they're impossible. When my son, Matthew, was born prematurely at just 27 weeks, weighing 2 pounds and 2 ounces, the world told me the odds were against us. Doctors painted a grim picture, and fear tried to creep into my heart. But through every sleepless night, tearful prayer, and whispered declaration of faith, I learned that God's promises are steadfast and His timing is perfect. This is the story of Matthew—a child who taught me to trust in God, fight with everything I had, and see beauty in the midst of trials. It's a story of how love, faith, and resilience can overcome the impossible. I hope that as you read this, you'll find the encouragement you need to face your own battles. Because no matter how hard life gets, I promise you, it's not for nothing.

Contents

My Life Purpose

I knew from a young age that I wanted to be something extraordinary. This was my biggest dream. I envisioned a life filled with purpose, where my hard work and faith would take me to places I had never been before. Moving to New York City alone was the first step toward that dream.

New York was everything and nothing like I had imagined. It was a city filled with limitless potential, where skyscrapers kissed the heavens, and ambition was a shared language. But I quickly realized that chasing greatness in a city as vast and unforgiving as New York required more than just big dreams—it required endurance, sacrifice, and an unwavering belief in myself. In that city, I was but a drop in a vast ocean of people, I had to push my way through and make it to the stop in order to stand out, to be something great. And I had to do it all on my own.

I didn't have the financial support of my parents to fall back on. This was unlike many of my peers who leaned on their families for help with rent, tuition, or even the smallest comforts. I stood on my own. There were no safety nets for me, no one to catch me when life knocked me down. Everything I had, I worked for. I had two jobs on top of school. This was not a choice for me; it was something I had to do. I needed the money, and I knew I had to manage two jobs if I wanted to continue living on my own in New York. Every dollar earned was carefully stretched to cover rent, tuition, and necessities. Was the weight of this burden drowning me? Certainly. There were moments when I wondered if I would ever catch up, if I could ever breathe without the weight of financial strain pressing down on me.

Despite the struggle, I made intentional choices to stay true to my values. In a world where many my age seemed to lose themselves in the chaos of the city—partying, drinking, smoking, or chasing fleeting relationships—I chose a different path. I wanted my life to mean something deeper. I sought to stay close to God, to live with integrity and discipline, even when the world around me felt like it was pulling me in every direction but the one I wanted to go. Yet, even in my pursuit of faith and purpose, I often felt as though I was falling short. I was putting in my all, but even my all was not enough.

Financial hardships plagued me no matter how hard I worked. It felt unfair at times—working two jobs, sacrificing sleep, and living with such strict discipline, only to feel like I was constantly on the edge of falling apart. The dream of becoming something great felt further and further away with each passing month. I questioned whether I was doing something wrong or if the world simply wasn't built for people like me—people without a safety net, without the privilege of support, trying to rise against all odds.

There were nights when I cried alone in my small apartment, the city lights outside my window reminding me of the life I was fighting for but hadn't yet reached. I carried the weight of my dreams alone, and at times, it felt like the burden might break me. But even in those moments of despair, I reminded myself why I started this journey in the first place. I wasn't just chasing greatness for myself—I wanted to prove that it was possible for someone like me, with no financial backing or shortcuts, to achieve something extraordinary. I also clung to my faith in God, though even that was a struggle. There were days when I questioned why God seemed so far away and why my prayers for provision and ease often seemed unanswered. But deep down, I knew that my journey was shaping me in ways I couldn't yet understand. I was learning resilience, independence, and strength. I was discovering my ability to persevere and to keep moving forward even when the odds were stacked against me. I moved forward, even if the step I took was small.

Through all the struggles, I've come to realize that greatness isn't always about achieving something grand or glamorous. Sometimes, it's found in the quiet moments of perseverance—choosing to keep going when everything in you wants to give up, staying true to your values in a world that tries to erode them, and holding onto faith when it feels like the hardest thing to do. My journey isn't over yet, and I know there will be more challenges ahead. But I've come this far on my own, and that is its own kind of greatness.

Looking back now, I see glimpses of that purpose in the strength I've gained through my struggles. Every rejection, every financial hardship, and every lonely night has taught me something about who I am. They've taught me to lean not on my own understanding but to trust in God's plan, even when it feels unclear. I've come to understand that His timing isn't always aligned with my own and that greatness might not look the way l imagined. God's purpose for my life may not be about the kind of success the world praises but about the person I'm becoming in the process. I've learned to stop defining my worth by my financial struggles or the milestones I haven't yet reached. Instead, I see the strength it takes to keep going as a victory in itself. The fact that I've stayed true to my values, held onto my faith, and continued to dream despite the odds is a reflection of God's work in me. I believe He is shaping me for something greater than I can understand right now.There are still days when I struggle to believe that brighter days are ahead. There are still moments when I feel like giving up. But in those times, I remind myself of God's promises.

Jeremiah 29:11 says, "For I know the plans I have for you, declares the Lord, plans to prosper you and not to harm you, plans to give you hope and a future." Those words remind me that my journey, with all its pain and uncertainty, is part of a greater story. Even when I feel lost, God is guiding me. Now, I view my struggles not as signs of failure but as stepping stones. Each challenge has brought me closer to understanding my resilience and dependence on God. God has a purpose for my life, and I trust that He is using every hardship to prepare me for something greater. My faith in Him is the foundation that keeps me grounded, even when the storms of life rage around me. So, I keep moving forward.

I don't have all the answers, and I don't know exactly where this path will lead. But I trust that my efforts, my faith, and my perseverance are not in vain. God has a purpose for my life, and as I continue to grow and learn, I know that purpose will become clearer. Until then, I'll keep striving to become the person He created me to be-faithful, resilient, and unshaken by the trials of this world.

One of my favorite quotes is, "A little faith will bring you to heaven, but a lot of faith will bring heaven to you." At first glance, this statement might seem like a contradiction, but it holds profound truth about the depth and impact of faith in our lives. A little faith is enough to guide us toward the promise of eternity, but when we cultivate a deeper, active, and abundant faith, it transforms our earthly lives in ways that mirror heaven here and now. It's a call to live beyond the basics of belief, to step into a faith that changes not only our eternal destiny but the world around us.

The idea that a little faith can bring us to heaven reflects the sufficiency of faith in God's grace. In Matthew 17:20, Jesus tells His disciples, "If you have faith as small as a mustard seed, you can say to this mountain, 'Move from here to there,' and it will move. Nothing will be impossible for you." A mustard seed is one of the smallest seeds, yet it grows into a towering tree. This imagery reminds us that even the smallest measure of faith is powerful enough to connect us to God's promises. For many, faith begins as something small—just enough to believe in God's existence, His love, and His plan for salvation. This kind of faith is often the starting point. It assures us that by believing in Jesus Christ, we are redeemed and have the hope of eternal life. It's a beautiful and foundational truth: salvation is not earned by the size of our faith but by the grace of God. Faith, no matter how small, opens the door to heaven. But what happens when faith doesn't stop at the threshold? What if we don't settle for the mustard seed but allow it to grow, mature, and flourish? That's where a lot of faith comes in—and where heaven begins to show up in our lives.

A lot of faith is different. It's not just about believing in the promise of heaven after death; it's about living in a way that reflects heaven on earth. When we choose to fully surrender our lives to God, to trust Him not only for our salvation but for every aspect of our lives, something profound happens. Faith ceases to be passive and becomes active. It becomes the lens through which we see the world, the fuel that drives our decisions, and the foundation upon which we build our lives. With abundant faith, we begin to experience God's presence, power, and peace in tangible ways. Heaven is no longer just a distant promise; it becomes a present reality. This kind of faith invites God's kingdom to invade our lives. In the Lord's Prayer, Jesus teaches us to pray, "Your kingdom come, Your will be done, on earth as it is in heaven." A lot of faith is what allows us to live out that prayer—to see God's kingdom at work here and now.

What Does Bringing Heaven to You Look Like?

1. Peace in the Midst of Chaos:

A lot of faith allows us to experience peace that surpasses all understanding, even in the most challenging circumstances. While the world around us may be in turmoil, faith grounds us in the assurance that God is in control. This peace is a glimpse of heaven, where there is no fear or anxiety.

2. Joy Despite Hardship:

Faith in abundance brings a joy that is not dependent on circumstances. It reminds us that our hope is rooted in something eternal. This joy radiates outward, touching the lives of those around us and creating a heavenly atmosphere wherever we go.

3. Transformation of Perspective:

A deep, abiding faith changes the way we see the world. Instead of being consumed by the temporary and material, we begin to focus on the eternal. We see people as God sees them, with love and compassion, and we find purpose in serving others. Heaven begins to shine in our actions and relationships.

A lot of faith is more than belief—it's an active, intentional relationship with God that transforms the way we live. It's a faith that doesn't just hope for miracles but expects them because it trusts in God's character and His promises. This deeper faith doesn't just change us on the inside; it begins to change the world around us. Heaven is brought to us because faith aligns our hearts and actions with God's will, inviting His presence into our daily lives.

I believe that a lot of faith compels us to act. James 2:17 says, "Faith by itself, if it is not accompanied by action, is dead." A little faith may bring us to the door of heaven, but it is faith in action—faith that is lived out in service, obedience, and trust—that allows heaven to touch the earth. This kind of faith looks like this:

• Loving the Unlovable:

Heaven on earth is reflected when we love others with the same grace and mercy that God shows us. A lot of faith enables us to forgive those who hurt us, to show kindness to strangers, and to extend compassion to those in need. When we love selflessly, we mirror God's heart, bringing His presence into the lives of others.

• Trusting God in the Unknown:

A lot of faith isn't afraid of uncertainty because it rests in the assurance that God is in control. It allows us to step out in obedience even when we don't see the whole path ahead. For example, think of Abraham, who left his home and everything he knew because God called him to. His faith brought him into a covenant relationship with God, where heaven's blessings touched his life and legacy.

•Living with Purpose:

When we have a lot of faith, we begin to see our lives as part of God's bigger plan. Every decision, no matter how small, becomes an opportunity to glorify Him. Whether it's excelling in our work, raising children with love and wisdom, or sharing our faith with others, we bring a little piece of heaven to earth when we live out our purpose with faith.

One of the most beautiful aspects of abundant faith is the way it brings us closer to God's presence. When our faith grows deeper, we begin to recognize His hand in every aspect of our lives. Heaven comes to us when we see His fingerprints in the beauty of a sunrise, the kindness of a stranger, or the peace that fills our hearts during prayer. The more we cultivate our faith, the more attuned we become to God's voice and His leading. We no longer feel alone in our struggles because we know He is walking with us. This nearness to God is a taste of heaven, where we will one day live in His presence fully and forever.

A lot of faith doesn't eliminate hardships, but it gives us the strength to endure them with hope. Heaven comes to us when we experience God's comfort in our pain and His guidance in our confusion. This kind of faith allows us to see trials not as obstacles but as opportunities for growth and reliance on God. Consider the story of Job. Despite losing everything—his wealth, family, and health—he never let go of his faith in God. In the end, Job's unwavering faith brought restoration and blessings that mirrored the abundance of heaven. His story reminds us that deep faith is not about avoiding suffering but about finding God's presence and purpose within it.

When we live with abundant faith, we don't just wait passively for heaven after death; we become agents of heaven here and now. This transformation can be seen in how we:

1. Impact Others:

A lot of faith inspires those around us. When people see us trusting God through difficult circumstances, loving others selflessly, or living with unshakable joy, they're drawn to the source of our faith. In this way, our lives become a reflection of heaven, pointing others toward God.

2. Change Our Communities:

Faith empowers us to make a difference in the world. Whether it's through acts of kindness, fighting for justice, or sharing the gospel, we bring heaven to earth by living out God's love in practical ways. The ripple effects of our faith can transform families, neighborhoods, and even nations.

3. Experience the Fruits of the Spirit:

Heaven is reflected in the fruits of the Spirit—love, joy, peace, patience, kindness, goodness, faithfulness, gentleness, and self-control. A lot of faith allows these qualities to flourish in our lives, making us more like Christ and bringing the atmosphere of heaven into our relationships and actions.

Ultimately, the difference between a little faith and a lot of faith is not about earning God's favor but about fully stepping into the life He offers us. A little faith connects us to God's grace, ensuring our place in heaven. But a lot of faith allows us to experience the fullness of His kingdom right now. It invites God to work in and through us, turning ordinary moments into glimpses of eternity. Heaven is not just a place we go to after death—it's a reality we can experience when we align our hearts and lives with God's will. Through abundant faith, we bring heaven closer to ourselves and to those around us. We live with the hope, peace, and joy of knowing that God's presence is with us, and that changes everything.

The Beginning

To best understand my journey through life, it is essential to start from the beginning, from my upbringing, presenting those who most shaped my life, my personality, my beliefs, and my faith.

I was born in Point De Sable, a small and vibrant island just outside Port-au-Prince, Haiti's bustling capital. Point De Sable was more than a place—it was a world of warmth and simplicity, where the sound of the ocean set the rhythm of daily life, and the stars blanketed us at night. My parents built our lives there, rooted in love and resilience. But like many families in Haiti, we faced challenges. When I was just a baby, my father left for the United States, taking my older sister with him in hopes of creating a better future for us all. This decision left my mother to raise me and my older sister alone, but she was a force of strength and determination.

Growing up, I didn't know my father. I had no memory of his face or the sound of his voice beyond the recordings on cassette tapes and brief phone calls. I would listen to his words, imagining what he looked like, longing for the day when we'd finally meet. That day came in 1988, eight years after he left. I still remember every detail of the moment my life changed. My mother woke us early and dressed my sister and me in our finest clothes. Our hair was neatly styled, adorned with the prettiest bows. I didn't know why the day felt special, but the excitement in my mother's voice gave it away. She wore her best dress and told us, "Today is an important day." When we arrived at the airport, I saw him. A light-skinned man with a smile that could brighten any room walked toward us. I hesitated at first, unsure if he was really the father I had imagined in my mind. But as he got closer, I knew. Without a second thought, I ran into his arms. For the first time in my life, I felt the safety and warmth of a father's embrace. Those years in Haiti were a mix of struggle and beauty. Life was simple, but joy was everywhere. Our home was less than a mile from the ocean, and sunsets painted the sky in hues of orange and pink. At night, the moon became our light, and the children in the neighborhood would gather outside. We'd sip on chocolate milk, eat bread, and listen as my cousin Marlene spun tales of mischievous dogs and clever cats. During Mardi Gras, the streets came alive with music and dancing. My mother forbade me from joining the parades, but the pull of the trumpets and drums was irresistible. I'd sneak out to dance, losing myself in the rhythm of the celebrations, only to face my mother's scolding when she found me.

As I grew older, life brought change. We moved from Point De Sable to Port-au-Prince, staying with my Aunt Bertha while my mother waited for my father to send money for a new home. Eventually, we settled in a house on Route Des Dalles, where life seemed to improve. I attended a prestigious private school, Gérard Gougue, and made friends in our new neighborhood. For a time, it felt like things were finally falling into place. But life had more transitions in store. My father sent for my mother and younger sister to join him in the United States, leaving me and my sister Samantha in the care of our Aunt Bertha. While I missed my mother terribly, my aunt became a second mother to us. She was kind and loving, and the village around us came together to help raise us.

The day I left Haiti was bittersweet. I was 15 years old, leaving behind everything I knew—my aunt, my friends, and the vibrant life of the island—to reunite with my parents in the United States. The excitement of seeing my family again was matched by the fear of the unknown. I remember landing in Miami, overwhelmed by the lights, the crowds, and the unfamiliar chill of winter. It was my first time feeling cold, and I immediately disliked it. From Miami, we flew to Orlando, where my new life began. Adjusting to life in America was harder than I had imagined. Everything felt foreign—the language, the food, the culture. I didn't speak English, and I struggled to find my place in this new world. My older sister and I leaned on each other during those early days, as we were all we had. It wasn't long before we met Elle, a girl who lived a few houses down. She became our first friend, introducing us to fast-food restaurants and shopping malls. She made the transition easier, showing us the small joys of life in America.

At home, life was strict. My father, though loving, ruled with firm discipline. I wasn't allowed to stay out late, go to the movies, or have sleepovers. Each time I pushed against the rules, I faced punishment, often in the form of a whooping. I didn't understand how he could love me so much yet discipline me so harshly. It created a distance between us that was hard to bridge. By 17, I was determined to gain independence. I got my first part-time job at Sears, saved money, and bought my first car—a little Toyota Celica. That car was my freedom, my first taste of adulthood. At 21, I moved to Tampa with a friend, embracing the thrill of living on my own. It was in Tampa that I met my first boyfriend at the age of 22. For the first time, I experienced love in a way that opened my heart, but life in Tampa didn't turn out as I had hoped. I eventually moved back to Orlando, got my first apartment, and tried to build a stable life. When finances became too tight, I returned to my parents' home, but the tension with my father remained. At 23, I made the bold decision to move to New York City, determined to carve out a new path for myself.

It was Christmas Eve, 2007, when I met the man who would change my life forever. A friend of mine, Daphne, had invited me to a holiday party. We weren't particularly close, so the invitation came as a surprise. I decided to go, even though I didn't know what to expect. The night of the party, I got lost trying to find the venue. As I wandered around, a tall, handsome man with a warm smile approached me. He had been watching me from a distance and asked if I needed help. His name was Gendry. He offered to guide me to the ballroom, but our conversation quickly turned into something deeper. By the end of the night, he asked for my number and invited me to dinner.

At first, I wasn't sure about him. I didn't return his calls right away. But something about Gendry lingered in my mind, and when I finally called him back, I was glad I did. Gendry was everything I had dreamed of in a partner—kind, ambitious, and deeply caring. He owned his own home, had a stable career, and carried himself with confidence. We started dating seriously, and Gendry quickly became a steady presence in my life. From the beginning, he made me feel safe and valued. At 26 years old, I felt like I had finally found someone who truly saw me.

After a year of dating, Gendry and I decided to move in together. We shared dreams of building a life and starting a family. But getting pregnant wasn't as easy as we had hoped. Gendry was diagnosed with a low sperm count, and we had to undergo insemination. When the insemination worked on the first try, we were ecstatic. I was finally pregnant, and the joy of knowing I was bringing life into the world was unlike anything I had ever felt. Gendry was over the moon, and he became the most supportive partner I could have asked for. During my first trimester, Gendry was attentive and caring, making sure I had everything I needed. We spent hours talking about the future, imagining what our child would be like. I felt like we were on the brink of something extraordinary.

But life had other plans. By the end of my first trimester, I started experiencing unbearable pain. Deep down, I knew something wasn't right. Late one night, I asked Gendry to take me to the emergency room. He reassured me that it was probably nothing, but I couldn't shake the feeling that something was wrong. The hospital dismissed my concerns and sent me home, but the pain persisted. When I returned the next day, I refused to leave until they gave me answers. After an ultrasound, the doctors discovered I had a short cervix and was at risk of preterm labor. I was admitted to the hospital immediately. The doctors recommended a cerclage, a procedure to keep the baby in my uterus. But even with the cerclage, they told me there was a 60% chance I might lose the baby. Their words hit me like a ton of bricks, but I refused to give up hope. I prayed fervently, believing that God would protect my child. Faith became my anchor, keeping me grounded as I faced the unknown.

The cerclage was successful, but I was placed on strict bed rest for the rest of my pregnancy. Gendry never left my side. After work, he would come to the hospital, bringing my favorite food and setting up movie nights to make me feel at ease. My family rallied around me as well—my mother, siblings, and in-laws all took turns visiting, making sure I never felt alone.

A Tiny Miracle

Despite all the precautions, I went into early labor at just 27 weeks. On September 24, 2009, my son, Matthew Angel Núñez, was born via C-section. He weighed only 2 pounds and 2 ounces, his tiny body fragile and vulnerable. The first time I saw him, my heart swelled with love and fear. He was so small, lying in the incubator, connected to machines that helped him breathe. I couldn't hold him, but I placed my hand inside and touched his little fingers. "Matthew," I whispered, "you are strong. God has a plan for you, and you're going to make it." The doctors told us that Matthew's lungs were underdeveloped and that his chances of survival were slim. He was placed on a ventilator, and we were told it would be a long journey. Every day, I sat by Matthew's side in the NICU, watching him fight for his life. The sound of monitors beeping became the soundtrack of my days. I prayed constantly, asking God to heal my son and give him the strength to keep fighting. The days were filled with small victories and setbacks. Some days, Matthew showed signs of improvement. Other days, his oxygen levels dropped, and the fear of losing him gripped my heart. At one point, he contracted RSV, a respiratory virus that made it even harder for him to breathe. The doctors told me there was little they could do. But I refused to accept their prognosis. I believed with every fiber of my being that God had the final say.

We met with the doctor, and I saw it in his eyes: the doubt, the fear.

Then, one night, I got the call every mother dreads.

The night doctor told me, "This is it. His lungs are too tired. If he stops breathing, we won't be able to resuscitate him because he's too little."

I refused to accept that.

I told the doctor, "Not my son. My son will live. I will walk out of this hospital with him when the time comes."

I immediately called my mother, sobbing, telling her what the doctor said.

She yelled at me.

"Stop crying. Get yourself together. You serve a mighty God. The same God who parted the Red Sea. The same God who raised the dead. He is the same God who is holding Matthew. Now go fight for your son."

That night, I wiped my tears and made a decision.

I was going to fight for Matthew.

The next day, Gendry and I went out and bought Matthew's car seat and started setting up his nursery.

I refused to plan for death. I planned for life.

I prayed over Matthew every single day. I didn't see him as a sick baby anymore, I saw him as a healthy, strong little boy. I envisioned him running in the grass, laughing, speaking, playing.

I refused to believe that this was the end.

Then, one day, something miraculous happened.

Gendry's sister, Jane, suggested we reach out to a lung specialist named Dr. Patel. The hospital had already mentioned a specialist, but they didn't believe it would make a difference.

We reached out anyway. Since Dr. Patel wasn't available, he sent Dr. Kapoor, who came to assess Matthew. She saw hope for Matthew and decided to start him on a special medication, believing it could make a difference. At first, she watched anxiously, unsure if it would have any effect, but within just a few days, a noticeable change began to take place. His strength slowly returned, his breathing grew steadier, and the exhaustion that had once dulled his eyes started to fade. It was as if a light had been reignited within him.

I spoke life over Matthew every single day. I laid my hands on his tiny chest, declaring, "You will breathe without help. You will grow strong. You will run and play like every other child." Gendry was my rock during this time. He visited Matthew every day, often spending hours by his side. Despite his own fears, he remained strong for me, reassuring me that our son would make it. The nurses and doctors in the NICU became like family. They cared for Matthew with such compassion, and I trusted them to do everything they could to help him. One nurse even told me, "Your son is a fighter. He's going to make it.

Bringing Matthew home after nine months in the NICU was a miracle I'll never forget. It was a moment I had prayed for every day, and when it finally happened, the joy was indescribable. Holding him in my arms as we walked out of the hospital felt like a victory—not just for him, but for all of us. But the journey wasn't over. Matthew still had challenges to overcome. He came home with a G-tube for feeding and needed oxygen support at night. These machines and routines became part of our daily lives, but I saw them as temporary obstacles, not permanent barriers. Every day, I laid my hands on Matthew and declared healing over his body. "You are whole. Your lungs will grow strong. You will eat and thrive, just like every other child." My faith never wavered, even when progress seemed slow.

Feeding was one of the biggest hurdles we faced. Matthew couldn't tolerate solid food and often vomited if we tried. The G-tube was his lifeline, but I was determined it wouldn't define his life. We worked closely with his speech and feeding therapists, who were patient and dedicated to helping him. I also prayed constantly, asking God to give Matthew the ability to eat like any other child. No matter how many times he threw up or refused food, I refused to give up. Slowly but surely, Matthew began to tolerate small amounts of solid food. Each tiny bite felt like a victory. Eventually, the vomiting stopped altogether, and we began to use the G-tube less and less. His pediatrician finally gave the green light to remove it, and though I was nervous about the surgery, I trusted God to see us through. Matthew came out of the procedure safe and sound. Watching him eat his first full meal on his own brought tears to my eyes. It was another testament to God's faithfulness.

Another milestone came when Matthew no longer needed oxygen support. For months, I prayed over his lungs, declaring life and strength into them. I visualized him running and playing outside without any machines holding him back. One day, his lung specialist told us that Matthew could start using the oxygen concentrator only at night. A few months later, he didn't need it at all. Seeing him breathe freely, without tubes or machines, was a moment of pure joy and relief.

When it was time for Matthew to start preschool, I was filled with both excitement and anxiety. I worried about him being away from me, about whether he'd be accepted and cared for. But once again, God provided. Matthew's teachers and therapists adored him, and he thrived in the new environment. His speech improved with time and practice, and his confidence began to grow. Still remember the first time he said, "Mama," with clarity. It was a moment I had prayed for, and when it happened, I cried tears of gratitude.

Through Matthew's journey, I learned that every challenge we face has a purpose. It's not always easy to see this in the moment, but God uses every trial to shape us, teach us, and prepare us for something greater. Before Matthew, I didn't know my purpose. I was just living, going through the motions of life. But his birth and the fight for his survival awakened something in me. I realized that my story—and Matthew's story—was meant to inspire others.

I believe that Matthew was part of God's plan to break the generational curses in our family. Through his life, I've seen the power of faith, resilience, and unconditional love. His journey has taught me to trust God completely and to declare victory, even in the face of uncertainty. As a mother, I wanted to protect Matthew from everything. I wanted to shield him from sickness, pain, and the harsh realities of life. But I realized that no matter how hard I tried, the only one who could truly protect him was God. Letting go was one of the hardest lessons I had to learn, but it was also one of the most freeing. When I released my fears and placed Matthew in God's hands, I found peace. Today, Matthew is a thriving young man with a bright future ahead of him. He is kind, compassionate, and deeply loved by everyone who knows him. He's an honor roll student, a loyal son, and a testament to the miracles that happen when we refuse to give up. Matthew has taught me more about faith and resilience than I ever thought possible. He's shown me that life's challenges are not meant to break us—they're meant to refine us.

It Wasn't for Nothing

If you're reading this, I want you to know that your struggles are not for nothing. Whatever you're going through, there is a purpose behind it. God hears your prayers, and He will come through for you in His perfect timing. Hold on to your faith. Keep praying, keep believing, and never give up. Remember, miracles still happen, and God's promises are unshakable. Matthew's life is proof of that. His journey has taught me that even in our darkest moments, there is always hope. So, if you're feeling weary, I encourage you to press on. Trust that God is working behind the scenes, and know that brighter days are ahead!

The Basket of Miracles:

There was one practice that aided me greatly in the tumultuous and painful time of my life when I was in the NICU almost every day. This practice is something I wish to share to display its effectiveness and ability to provide strength in times when all seems lost and you begin losing faith. I know that this helped me when I was nothing but terrified and anxious, when I questioned whether my son could live and become a happy, healthy boy.

When Matthew was born prematurely, the doctors immediately whisked him away to the Neonatal Intensive Care Unit (NICU). The days that followed were filled with anxiety, uncertainty, and an overwhelming sense of helplessness. As a parent, watching your child struggle to breathe and fight for their life is an experience that shakes the very foundation of your being. In those moments of despair, I turned to the one source of strength that has always been my anchor: my faith in God.

In the midst of our trials, I decided to create a tangible reminder of God's presence and faithfulness—a basket at home where I would place a small rock for every answered prayer. It was a modest idea, but it held profound significance. Each rock represented a moment of divine intervention, a testament to the power of prayer and the goodness of God.

Every time I prayed for Matthew's healing, for his strength, for the wisdom of the medical staff, and for our family's endurance, I placed a rock in the basket. It became a ritual, a sacred act of trust and hope. The basket, initially empty, began to fill with these little tokens of faith, each one a symbol of a prayer heard and answered.

The NICU can be a place of miracles and heartbreaks. For us, it became a sanctuary where we witnessed the miraculous power of God's grace. There were days when Matthew's condition improved unexpectedly, when his tiny body responded to treatments and his vital signs stabilized. Each of these moments felt like a divine whisper, a gentle reassurance that God was with us.

I remember vividly the day when Matthew opened his eyes for the first time, the day he no longer needed the ventilator, and the day he finally gained enough weight to be moved out of the incubator. These milestones were more than just medical achievements; they were answered prayers, miracles in their own right. Each time we received good news, I would rush home to place another rock in the basket, my heart swelling with gratitude. As the days turned into weeks, the basket grew heavier with rocks. It stood as a silent witness to our journey of faith, each stone a chapter in our story of hope and resilience. By the time Matthew was ready to come home, the basket was filled to the brim. It was a visual representation of our spiritual journey, a testament to the countless ways God had shown His compassion and love. Bringing Matthew home was an emotional moment, one that I will cherish forever. The sight of that overflowing basket brought tears to my eyes. It was a powerful reminder of God's unwavering goodness, a tangible proof of His mercy and grace. Every rock in that basket told a story of a prayer answered, a miracle witnessed, and a heart filled with gratitude.

The basket of rocks now holds a place of honor in our home. It serves as a constant reminder of God's faithfulness, a symbol of hope in times of trouble, and a source of inspiration for our family. Whenever we face challenges or uncertainties, we look at that basket and remember the miracles we have witnessed, the prayers that have been answered, and the grace that has been bestowed upon us. Matthew's journey in the NICU taught us the true meaning of faith and the incredible power of prayer. It showed us that even in the darkest moments, God's light shines through, offering protection, comfort, and hope. The basket of rocks is more than just a collection of stones; it is a testament to the transformative power of faith and the boundless compassion of our Creator.

Now, I am filled with profound gratitude for the grace and mercy we have experienced. The basket of rocks stands as a legacy of faith that we will carry with us always, a symbol of hope that continues to inspire and strengthen us.

My Relationship with my Father

Each leg of my life's journey has made me into the woman I am today, whose faith is endless and enduring. One of the most important of these was when I moved from Haiti to America. During this time, there was one person whose influence shaped me the most: my father.

When I found out that I was coming to the United States to live with my father and mother—it felt like a gift. I couldn't wait for that day to arrive. My sister Samantha and I were inseparable, and both of our parents made sure we came to the United States together. If one of us had received a visa before the other, it would have crushed us both.

To this day, I still remember vividly the moment I first set foot on American soil. I was 15 years old, and my sister was 16. We had promised each other and God that we would make something of ourselves and always keep Him at the center of our lives.

My father was very strict. His first talk with us was about how we weren't allowed to have friends. The only things we were allowed to do were go to school, church, and come home. I thought this was strange, especially since I was so outgoing. For me, this rule felt like an impossible task.

On our first day of high school, we met a girl who lived next door. My sister and I quickly became friends with her. She was kind, and over time, she became like a sister to us. However, my father strictly forbade the friendship. Even at 15, I felt I had the right to make my own decisions. This led to many back-and-forth arguments with my dad. It was during this time that the discipline escalated, and the whooping began. From that point on, my relationship with my father started to change.

The more I was forbidden from having friends, the more I sought them out. Though I could only talk to them on the phone since going out was forbidden, I was constantly on the phone—either with friends from work or church. When my friend invited me to her boyfriend's birthday party, I was almost 18 years old. I was terrified to ask my father for permission because I knew the answer would be no. I waited until my parents went to bed and snuck out of the house.

When my father found out what I had done, he waited until my mother left for work and beat me in a rage until he was too tired to continue. I was left with bruises all over my body. I couldn't tell anyone because I was afraid my father would go to jail. That incident was the beginning of my battle with depression, and it completely destroyed my relationship with my father.

I know my father loved me, but he didn't know how to show it. I would hear stories about how his own father had beaten him so badly as a child that he lost hearing in one ear. The trauma my father endured was potentially being passed down to me. For a long time, I thought my father hated me. Even though he provided a home, a warm meal, and financial stability, his actions made me believe otherwise.

My father's job was to protect me, guide me, and keep me safe—not to hit me so hard that I was left bruised and broken. Years later, I asked my father, "How can you say you love me when you used to make me cry?" His response was, "If I wasn't that way with you, you wouldn't be where you are right now. You wouldn't be this incredible woman."

What my father failed to understand was that I was just a young woman trying to find my way in this world, and I needed him every step of the way. So I grew up hating my father, and our relationship was never the same. Whenever he was home, I would stay in my room all day, too terrified to come out. I counted the days until I turned 18 so I could leave for college and finally escape.

I promised that I would never be like my father. I vowed to love, respect, and protect my child in ways I wished I had been protected. From the moment my son, Matthew, was born, my heart was filled with a love I never knew existed. I wanted to give him everything I didn't have—a safe, nurturing, and loving environment where he would feel cherished every single day.

One time, when he was little, I spanked him. The moment he cried, it shattered me. It brought back memories of my own childhood—the pain and fear I felt when my father beat me—and I immediately knew I could never do that again. That experience strengthened my resolve to be a different kind of parent—one who disciplines with patience and understanding, not anger or force.

My love for Matthew taught me so much about healing and breaking cycles. He's my greatest joy, my biggest blessing, and my daily reminder that love, kindness, and gentleness are the most powerful tools a parent can have. Watching him grow into the person he is today fills my heart with pride and gratitude. Every laugh, every hug, and every moment we share is a testament to the promise I made long ago—to always love my child in a way that makes him feel safe, valued, and deeply loved.

I didn't forgive my father for a very long time. The pain he caused me left deep emotional scars that I carried for years. Every time I thought about the way he disciplined me, the way his anger turned into physical punishment and the fear that consumed me in his presence, it was impossible to let go of the resentment. I couldn't reconcile the love I wanted from him with the hurt he inflicted on me. Even though he provided a home, food, and financial stability, the lack of emotional connection and the harshness of his actions overshadowed everything else. I felt betrayed by the person who was supposed to protect me, and that betrayal festered inside me, turning into anger, sadness, and bitterness. I would replay those memories over and over, questioning how someone who claimed to love me could also be the source of so much pain. For years, I avoided him, not just physically but emotionally, keeping a wall between us because it felt safer that way. I told myself that forgiving him would mean excusing his actions, and I wasn't ready to do that. The thought of forgiveness felt like letting go of the justice I thought I deserved. It wasn't until I began to understand his own pain and the generational cycle of trauma that I started to soften, but even then, forgiveness didn't come quickly or easily. It was a process that required me to face my own hurt and decide if I was ready to let go of the burden I had been carrying for so long.

Even though my father disciplined me harshly, I always admired his drive and determination, and deep down, I wanted to be as successful as him. Despite the pain and the strict rules, I couldn't overlook the fact that he was a hardworking man who built many businesses from the ground up. He provided for our family and created a stable life through his relentless effort and vision. As I grew older, I began to see that his discipline, though extreme, came from a place of wanting us to be strong, resilient, and successful in our own lives. I may not have agreed with his methods, but his work ethic and achievements inspired me to dream big and work hard. In many ways, his success became a blueprint for me, not just in building a career but in understanding the importance of perseverance and dedication.

I often wonder what kind of trauma my father went through that caused him to behave the way he did with us, his children. I've heard bits and pieces about his childhood, how his own father was harsh to him, how he lost his mother in his early 20s, and how he grew up in an environment where love was rarely shown. It makes me question what he must have endured emotionally and physically and how those experiences shaped the man he became. Was he taught that discipline had to come through fear and control? Was he ever given the space to heal or to express his pain? I think about how he carried the weight of his past into his role as a father, perhaps not even realizing how much it affected his actions.

I wonder if he believed that the way he raised us was the only way to prepare us for life or if he was simply repeating the patterns he had known all his life. It hurts to think that he, too, might have been a victim of his circumstances, trapped in a cycle of trauma that he didn't know how to break. While it doesn't excuse the pain he caused, it helps me see him through a more compassionate lens, as someone who was shaped by his own struggles and upbringing. Sometimes, I wish I could go back in time and understand his story better, to see the boy he once was before life hardened him, and to tell him that it's okay to choose a different path.

I know My father's journey to the United States is something I've thought about often, and the more I reflect on it, the more I realize how hard it must have been for him. He left his wife and children behind, traveling by boat to a foreign country with nothing but hope and determination to build a better future for his family. I can't imagine the emotional toll it must have taken on him to say goodbye to his loved ones, knowing he wouldn't see us for years. He must have been consumed by a mix of fear, loneliness, and an overwhelming sense of responsibility to succeed not for himself but for us.

Starting over in a new country with no support system and no guarantees takes incredible courage. He faced countless struggles and uncertainties, working tirelessly to establish a stable life while carrying the weight of his family's future on his shoulders. I think about the sacrifices he made, the long hours he worked, and the challenges he endured so that one day, we could join him and have a chance at a better life. While his choices may have caused pain and separation, I've come to understand that they were made out of love and a deep desire to give us opportunities he never had. His journey was not just physical; it was emotional, a testament to his strength and resilience, and I've grown to appreciate the magnitude of what he did for us.

I think that everyone has a story, a unique journey that shapes who they are and how they see the world. Behind every face is a history filled with triumphs, struggles, heartbreaks, and victories that most people may never know. Some stories are filled with joy, laughter, and love, while others are marked by pain, resilience, and survival. Every decision we make, every experience we live through, adds a chapter to our story. It's easy to judge someone based on what we see on the surface, but beneath that exterior lies a complexity we can't fully comprehend. The quiet person in the room might carry a history of loss, the loudest voice may be masking insecurities, and the person who seems to have it all together may have fought unimaginable battles to get there. Our stories connect us, remind us of our humanity, and show us that even though we each walk a different path, we share the same hopes, dreams, and desire to be understood. Every person you meet is living their own narrative, filled with lessons, scars, and moments of growth. To truly know someone, you have to listen to their story, and when you do, you may find pieces of your own reflected in theirs.

I often wish I could go back and truly understand my father's story, to sit with him and give him the space to open up about his teenage years and the experiences that shaped him. I wonder what kind of life he lived as a young man—what he dreamed of, what he feared, and whether he ever faced hardships that left a lasting mark on him. Did he experience love and kindness, or was he constantly met with discipline and survival? Was there someone in his life who inspired him, or did he have to find his own way through trial and error? These are questions I'll probably never fully have answers to, but I wish I had asked him. Maybe if we'd had that conversation, I could have seen beyond the strict, distant father I grew up with and instead understood the human being beneath the surface, the boy who had dreams, faced struggles, and possibly endured pain he never learned how to talk about.

I think about how hard it must have been for him to carry his past, whatever it was, while raising a family and trying to provide for us. Perhaps he didn't know how to process his emotions or break free from the cycle of trauma he might have endured. If I could go back, I'd ask him to share his story, not to excuse his actions but to connect with him in a way I never had the chance to. I'd want him to know that he could speak freely, without judgment, and that his story mattered because understanding it might have brought us closer and given me insight into the man behind the father.

Although I've only been in relationships with three men, I've noticed a pattern that's hard to ignore: I tend to be drawn to men who have the same personality traits as my father. It's not something I intentionally sought out, and it wasn't even obvious to me at first, but over time, I realized the similarities. These men often carried themselves with the same authority, stubbornness, and emotional distance that I grew up with. Like my father, they had strong personalities, a need for control, and a way of making me feel small during arguments. When I analyze this in hindsight, I can see how my childhood shaped the kind of love I accepted and thought I deserved. It's as if I subconsciously gravitated toward what felt familiar, even if it wasn't always healthy. There were moments in these relationships where I felt trapped in a cycle of seeking approval, trying to prove my worth, or walking on eggshells to avoid conflict, just as I had done with my father. It's a painful realization, but it's also been eye-opening because it's helped me understand how unresolved pain from my upbringing has influenced my choices. Recognizing this pattern has been the first step toward breaking it, and it's taught me the importance of healing and setting boundaries so I can choose partners who bring out the best in me rather than echoing the struggles of my past. It has also taught me just how much my behaviors and actions are going to impact my own son, with how I treat him being reflected in his own choice of partners. This realization has made me strive to treat him well all the time, to ensure that he knows what he deserves and what he is worth. I make sure I show my son respect and love so that these are things he does not lack later in life in his relationships with others and with himself.

I want to be the kind of woman who sets an example of love, strength, and grace for my son—a woman who teaches him, through my actions, what to look for in a good wife. I want him to see in me someone who is kind and compassionate, someone who speaks with gentleness but carries herself with confidence. I want him to remember how I treated others with respect and integrity, how I valued honesty, and how I always stood firm in my beliefs while remaining open-minded and understanding. I want to show him the importance of patience and forgiveness, not just in how I interact with him but in how I handle life's challenges. By being a nurturing and supportive mother, I hope to teach him the value of choosing a partner who will uplift him and walk alongside him, not behind or ahead of him. I want him to see how I balance love with boundaries and strength with vulnerability, so he learns to appreciate a woman who is both tender and resilient. Most of all, I want him to see how deeply I value and love him so he knows that he deserves a woman who will love him with the same devotion and care. If I can live my life as a reflection of these qualities, I believe it will guide him toward finding a partner who will help him build a strong, loving, and fulfilling marriage. These are all things I sorely lacked, and they festered in me, driven by my history and relationship with my father as well as the events I experienced regarding him. Despite it all, I knew that I deeply cared for and loved my father.

When I found out my father had cancer, a wave of emotions hit me all at once. It was as if time stood still, and I didn't know how to process what I was feeling. There was shock, fear, sadness, and even confusion. Despite the hurt and anger I had carried for so long, the news of his illness stirred something deep within me. It reminded me of the fragile nature of life and how fleeting time can be. I thought about the years we had spent apart emotionally, the walls I had built, and all the unresolved feelings between us. Part of me was overwhelmed with guilt... guilt for not forgiving him sooner, for the distance I had kept, and for the moments we had lost. Another part of me felt sadness, not just for the fact that he was sick, but for the broken relationship we never truly repaired. Yet, I also felt a strange tenderness, a longing to be there for him in a way he might not have been for me. It was as if all the pain of the past was suddenly eclipsed by the reality of the present. I realized that whatever time we had left was precious, and holding onto anger no longer felt important. Instead, I felt the need to show him love, to let go of the bitterness, and to focus on what truly mattered making the most of whatever time we had left together. Seeing my father in the hospital after months of not talking was an overwhelming experience, filled with a flood of emotions I didn't fully know how to process. As I walked into the room and saw him lying there, looking frail and vulnerable, it was like time stopped. The man I had always seen as strong and unyielding was now someone who seemed small and fragile. I felt a mix of sadness, guilt, and even anger—not at him, but at the years of distance and unresolved pain between us. Part of me wanted to run to his side, hold his hand, and tell him I loved him, while another part felt the weight of all the things we had left unsaid. I thought about all the arguments, the hurt, and the silence that had created a rift between us, and suddenly, none of it seemed as important as the reality in front of me. Seeing him in that state reminded me of how fleeting life can be and how much time we had lost. My heart ached with a longing to reconnect, to let go of the resentment, and to just be present for him. In that moment, all I wanted was for him to know that, despite everything, I still cared deeply for him, and I hoped it wasn't too late to bridge the gap between us.

Hearing that my father had stage 4 cancer on top of dementia felt like a punch in the gut. Everything I'd known about him—his strength, his stubborn will, and even the complicated history between us—suddenly came into sharper focus. I felt overwhelmed by a rush of emotions: fear, grief, regret, and a deep sadness that all the unresolved tension in our relationship might now be overshadowed by an illness we couldn't control. The doctor's words echoed in my mind, leaving me grappling with the reality that his time might be limited and that the future was going to be filled with new challenges. A part of me wanted to hold on to the father I remembered, even though that memory was complicated, while another part ached knowing we might never find the closure or reconciliation I once hoped for. As I processed this news, I realized how vital it was to find compassion, both for him and for myself. Despite the difficult history we shared, I couldn't ignore the fact that he was still my father, and now, more than ever, he needed understanding, support, and love.

From the very beginning, I made it a priority to take my father to all of his doctors' appointments, wanting to personally oversee his care and ensure he received the best possible treatment. However, as his health demands grew and my own responsibilities piled up, taking care of my son, running my business, and managing a household, I began to feel overwhelmed. That's when I made the difficult decision to hire a caregiver for him. It wasn't easy to hand over part of his day-to-day care to someone else, but I realized I needed help to balance my father's needs with my own family and work obligations. Even though I was no longer with him around the clock, I stayed involved by speaking to him regularly and visiting him every week. Knowing he had professional support gave me peace of mind, and these weekly visits allowed me to maintain our bond and make sure he felt loved, supported, and never forgotten.

Looking back on everything, I realize just how much I've grown and what I've truly learned. I've seen firsthand how deeply our past can shape us and how cycles of pain and trauma can get passed down if we're not careful. My father's strict upbringing and his struggles with showing love became lessons for me not just about what I wanted to avoid, but about the power of empathy and understanding. Caring for him in his sickness, despite our complicated history, taught me that there's a certain beauty in choosing compassion, even when anger or resentment would be easier. I learned that taking care of someone else, especially a parent who once hurt you, doesn't erase the past, but it can create a space for healing and forgiveness. I also discovered the importance of balance, realizing that I can't pour from an empty cup; I have to tend to my own emotional needs, my child, and my work, and that sometimes means asking for help. Above all, I learned that life is fragile and painfully short. Holding onto bitterness only weighs you down, and sometimes the greatest kindness you can give to yourself and to someone who's hurt you is to let go of the anger and offer love in whatever capacity you can.

It's only now, after all these years of wrestling with my father's harsh discipline, that I can look back and see how much his strictness helped shape the woman I am today. While it was painful at times and created wounds that took years to heal, it also instilled in me a resilience and determination that I might not have developed otherwise. His high expectations taught me not to settle for mediocrity, and his relentless drive for success showed me how far hard work and dedication can truly take a person. Even though I once resented the way he pushed me, I can see now that his intensity forced me to look within myself and find a strength I never knew existed. It's because of his toughness that I learned to stand on my own feet, to chase my goals, and to never give up when life throws challenges my way. In many ways, my success today is a testament to the lessons he imparted, both the good and the hard ones, which ultimately shaped me into the determined, capable woman I have become.

Through it all, I believe God was teaching me about the power of grace, forgiveness, and unconditional love. Even in the midst of anger and hurt, He showed me how important it is to open my heart and care for someone who once caused me pain. I realized that forgiveness isn't about excusing wrongdoings, but rather about freeing myself from the weight of bitterness and letting God's love fill the spaces where resentment once thrived. God reminded me that healing can happen in the most unexpected ways—by tending to my father in his time of need, I found a depth of empathy and compassion I didn't know I possessed. He also taught me the value of humility, showing me that it's okay to seek help and lean on others when life becomes overwhelming. Most of all, I learned that no matter how broken a relationship may seem, there is always room for grace, and in choosing kindness, we reflect the very heart of God's love. Looking back, I see just how many lessons my family and their experiences taught me, shaping the way in which I viewed the world.

Alexandra: A Heart of Gold

Alexandra was born in September 1988. I was 8 years of age when she was born, and I still remember the day vividly. It was a moment that changed our family forever. She came into the world naturally, and from the moment my mother held her in her arms, it was clear that she was special. The day my mother brought her home was one of the happiest moments of my life. **Alexandra** was the sweetest and cutest baby, with soft brown skin and the most beautiful eyes I had ever seen. There was something about her presence that immediately filled our home with warmth and joy. Having another sister was a blessing, and I felt an instant connection to her.

As she grew, **Alexandra**'s personality shone even brighter. She had a tenderness that was rare, a heart so pure that anyone who met her could see the goodness in her soul. She was always full of love, always ready to give. Even as a child, she had a way of making everyone feel special, as if she could sense what was in our hearts. I adored her deeply, and there was a part of me that felt responsible for her, even though I was still young myself.

When my father sent for my mother, **Alexandra** went with her. It was painful to be separated from them, but at the time, I believed it was temporary. I never imagined how much I would miss her, nor did I realize how long it would be before I saw her again. Life had a way of pulling us in different directions, but no matter where we were, my love for **Alexandra** never faded.

Years passed before I finally reunited with her in the United States. That moment is one I will never forget. Seeing her again after so much time apart was emotional beyond words. She had grown into a beautiful young woman, kind and full of grace, just as I had always imagined she would.

Despite the years and the distance, our bond remained unbroken. It was as if no time had passed at all.

At that time, adjusting to life in a new country was challenging. We did not know English, and everything felt unfamiliar. But **Alexandra**, with her gentle nature, stepped in to help us. She was patient, understanding, and always willing to support us in any way she could. She made sure we never felt alone, even in a place that was so new to us. That was just the kind of person she was—selfless and loving, always putting others before herself.

I thought about how she had been in good hands while I was away, growing up with both of our parents. I believed that she was safe, loved, and protected. But I guess I was wrong. Life is not always what it seems, and sometimes the people we trust to care for us the most can also be the ones who fail us in ways we never expected.

When my sister told me what had happened, when she said that our own father had touched her inappropriately, not just once, but multiple times, I felt like the air had been ripped from my lungs. My mind refused to believe it. Not him. Not our father. It was as if the ground beneath me had collapsed, leaving me in free fall, unable to grasp onto anything solid. A flood of emotions hit me all at once—anger, sorrow, disbelief, and an overwhelming sense of helplessness. How could someone who was supposed to love and protect us do something so horrific? The weight of those words, of her pain, settled deep inside me, and I felt shattered. I wanted to take it all away, to erase every moment of suffering she had endured. But I couldn't. And that broke me even more.

I replayed memories in my mind, searching for signs I had missed. Had there been moments when she needed me, but I didn't see it? Had she carried this pain alone for so long, afraid to speak? The thought of her suffering in silence tore me apart. More than anything, I wanted to hold her, to tell her she was not alone, that I would never let her go through this without me. I wanted her to know that this was not her fault, that she was still whole, still worthy of love and safety. And yet, beneath it all, a rage burned inside me, an anger so fierce that it scared me. Because no one, especially not our father, had the right to take away her sense of security, her innocence, her trust. That moment changed everything. It altered the way I saw my past, my family, and even myself. But if there was one thing I knew with absolute certainty, it was that I would stand by her, no matter what. I would be her safe place, her voice when she felt unheard, her strength when she felt weak. Because no one should have to carry this burden alone.

The moment I learned the truth, I knew I couldn't stay silent. I booked a flight from New York City to Florida, my mind racing the entire way. I wasn't going there for comfort, I was going to confront my father, to demand answers for the unimaginable pain he had caused. Sitting on the plane, my emotions swung between rage and disbelief. How could he do this? How could he betray the very people he was meant to protect? I replayed everything in my mind, searching for the right words, though I knew no words could ever make sense of what he had done.

When I finally stood before him, I felt the weight of years of trust shattering in that moment. I looked him in the eyes, demanding the truth, demanding accountability. He had taken something that could never be undone, and I refused to let him hide from it. When I arrived at my father's house, I felt an eerie calm wash over me, masking the storm inside. I had spent the entire flight rehearsing what I would say, but standing there in front of him, all of those words disappeared. Instead, all that remained was raw, unfiltered emotion.

"Tell me the truth," I demanded, my voice shaking but firm. "How long has this been happening? How could you do this?"

He didn't even flinch. His face remained expressionless, as if I were speaking nonsense, as if **Alexandra's** suffering was something he could dismiss like it never happened. He didn't deny it outright, nor did he acknowledge it. Instead, he simply refused to answer. That silence was louder than any confession. My anger erupted. "You don't get to ignore this!" I shouted, my voice trembling with rage. "She was a child! Your own daughter! You were supposed to love and protect her, and instead, you—" My voice broke before I could finish.

Still, he said nothing. No guilt. No remorse. No explanation.

I felt sick. I had come looking for answers, for some kind of reckoning, but all I found was a coward—a man too weak to even admit to his own monstrous actions. I kept pushing. I wanted him to say something, anything that would at least show he understood the depth of what he had done. But instead of giving me the truth, he did something I never expected.

He called the police.

I watched in disbelief as he picked up the phone and calmly reported that I was trespassing, that I was being aggressive, that he felt unsafe. The audacity of it all left me speechless. After everything he had done, after all the lives he had shattered, he was trying to paint himself as the victim. I didn't move. I didn't run. Let them come. I had nothing to hide.

Minutes later, the police arrived, their flashing lights illuminating the driveway. I stood my ground, ready to defend myself, ready to explain everything. But before I could even speak, something happened that I hadn't anticipated.

The officers didn't just look at me. They looked at him. And then, something shifted.

They weren't here for me.

They were here for him.

I watched as their demeanor changed, as they turned to my father with suspicion. They must have known something wasn't right. Maybe it was the way I stood my ground. Maybe it was the rage in my eyes, the desperation in my voice. Or maybe, just maybe, they already knew who he was. Then, before I could process what was happening, I saw it, the moment justice finally caught up to him.

They arrested him.

For a second, time seemed to stop. My father, the man I had once looked up to, the man I had loved despite his flaws, was now being handcuffed and taken away. There was no escaping the truth now. He could no longer hide behind silence, behind denial. I wanted to feel relief. I wanted to believe that this was the moment everything would be set right. But as I stood there, watching them take him away, all I felt was exhaustion. This wasn't the end. This was just the beginning. Because justice, as necessary as it was, would never erase the scars **Alexandra** carried. It wouldn't undo the years of pain or silence. But at least now, finally, he couldn't hurt her or anyone else ever again.

The Truth That Was Silenced

My father went to jail for over a month. For the first time, it felt like justice was finally within reach. But that hope was short-lived. My mother, determined to protect him, hired the top lawyer in the city. The weight of the case shifted, and then came the moment that changed everything—my little sister, just 14 years old, recanted her story. She told them she had lied.

I couldn't believe it. I sat there, trying to process what had just happened. Why would she lie? Why would she take it all back after everything she had been through? Deep inside, though, I knew the answer. She hadn't lied to me before. She had been forced to lie now. She was just a child, caught in the middle of something far bigger than she could handle. And in the end, she did what she thought she had to do. With her retraction, my father was released. And my mother—who should have stood by her daughter, made a choice that broke me even more. She sent **Alexandra** away and chose to stay with my father. It was as if she had erased **Alexandra** from our family, as if protecting him mattered more than protecting her. From that moment on, things were never the same.

I wanted **Alexandra** to live her life without this weight dragging her down. So, I never brought it up again. But that silence didn't mean I forgot. It haunted me for years because I knew she had been telling the truth. Years later, when I finally asked her why she had lied to save our father, her answer shattered me all over again. "He was the breadwinner," she said. "If he went to jail for life, how would our mother take care of me and our two brothers?"

She had sacrificed herself for them. At just 14 years old, she had been forced to carry a burden no child should ever bear, to choose between her own truth and the survival of our family.

Years later, **Alexandra** confronted our father. And for the first time, he admitted what he had done. He apologized to her. But that wasn't enough for me. An apology could never erase the years of pain, the betrayal, the stolen innocence. It could never make up for the fact that the one person who was supposed to protect her had been the one to destroy her trust. The only true justice would have been for him to be held accountable for what he did for him to truly pay for his actions. But that never happened. Instead, **Alexandra** carried the weight of it all, the pain, the silence, the betrayal. She went on with life, but she was never the same. Because how could she be? The people who were supposed to protect her had failed her. And no apology could ever change that.

A Lesson in Forgiveness

When my father was diagnosed with dementia and cancer, I wasn't sure how to feel. The man who had caused so much pain, who had shattered the trust of those who loved him, was now vulnerable, facing an illness that no one could escape. I knew I had to tell Alexandra. Despite everything, she had a right to know.

When I called her and told her the news, her response stunned me. "Let me know if you need help with him. I am willing to help." I couldn't believe what I was hearing. The same man who had caused her so much suffering was now sick, and her first instinct was to offer help. How? How could she have the strength to do that? How could she extend kindness to the very person who had stolen so much from her? It was in that moment that I realized **Alexandra** was teaching me something profound, something I hadn't yet grasped. Forgiveness.

Forgiveness isn't about the person who hurt you. It isn't about excusing what they did or pretending it never happened. It's about you. It's about choosing not to let the pain control you, not allowing the past to steal your future. **Alexandra** understood something that took me years to fully comprehend.

Jesus teaches us to forgive those who hurt us—not because they deserve it, but because holding onto bitterness only chains us to the pain. **Alexandra** didn't forgive because our father earned it; she forgave because she refused to let his actions define her. She chose peace over resentment. Her strength, her grace, left me in awe. And while I may not have been ready to offer the same forgiveness, I knew that in her heart, she had already found the freedom that forgiveness brings. **Alexandra's** story shattered me into pieces, yet, at the same time, it gave me strength. It opened my eyes to a painful truth: Sometimes, the very people who are meant to protect us are the ones who hurt us the most. The father who should have been her shield became the source of her deepest wounds. The mother who should have given unconditional love turned away. The friends we trust sometimes betray us. But through it all, there is one truth that remains unshaken—there is One who will never leave us nor forsake us. His name is Jesus Christ. If that's not hope, I don't know what is.

My bond with **Alexandra** is something I cherish beyond words. She is the kind of sister everyone should have in their life, loyal, selfless, and willing to protect others, even at the cost of herself. Her strength, her resilience, and her ability to love despite the pain inspire me every day. **Alexandra's** strength and resilience taught me something I never thought I would feel again: that our heart could beat again, that we could find hope and healing even after the deepest of wounds. For so long, I was consumed by the pain of what happened, unable to move past the betrayal and hurt. But **Alexandra**, despite everything she had been through, showed me that it was possible to heal, to forgive, and to rediscover the capacity for love.

Through her, I learned that even in the darkest moments, there is a way forward. She taught me that the heart, no matter how broken, can heal. And in her forgiveness, in her courage, I saw my own heart begin to beat again.

I pray that healing, joy, and blessings follow her all the days of her life. May she always walk in light, surrounded by the love and peace she so deeply deserves.

Samantha and I

My relationship with Samantha was always so unique, the kind of bond that felt more like destiny than chance. She was the sister I had always longed for—the one who understood me in ways no one else could. With her, there was an unspoken connection, a deep sense of trust and love that made every moment together feel special. She wasn't just a sister by relation; she was a sister by heart, the kind of person who supported me, laughed with me, and made life feel lighter. Our bond was more than just family—it was a rare and beautiful friendship that I will always cherish. Our relationship was different. There were times that I couldn't go to sleep without her—it was as if her presence brought me a sense of peace and comfort that nothing else could. Just knowing she was there made me feel safe, like everything was right in the world. Whether it was her voice, her laugh, or simply the warmth of her being nearby, it became a part of my nightly routine, something I depended on to settle my mind and heart. Without her, the silence felt heavier, and sleep just wouldn't come as easily. She was more than my sister; she was my sense of home and calm, and I couldn't rest without her by my side.

Samantha was a young, quiet girl, the kind of person who seemed to observe the world more than speak about it. She carried a calm presence, often lost in her own thoughts, yet there was a depth to her silence that made you curious about what she was thinking. Her quietness wasn't out of shyness but more a reflection of her introspective nature. She didn't need to say much to leave an impression—her actions, her gentle demeanor, and the way she carried herself spoke volumes. She was the kind of person who found peace in stillness, and her quiet strength was something I deeply admired.

Samantha and I were inseparable—we went to school together, studied together, and did everything side by side.

From walking to class to staying up late and helping each other prepare for exams, we shared every part of our daily lives. Whether it was tackling schoolwork, laughing at something silly, or simply sitting quietly in each other's presence, everything felt easier and more meaningful because we were together. She wasn't just my sister; she was my constant companion, my teammate, and my greatest support. Whatever we did, we faced it as a team, and those moments became some of the most cherished memories of my life. I always thought Samantha and I would be inseparable, that no matter where life took us, we'd never be apart. But then the unthinkable happened, something I never imagined or prepared for. Life had a way of pulling us in different directions, creating a distance I never thought possible between us. It was as if a piece of me was missing, and the bond we had always shared felt painfully distant. I never thought I'd have to face a reality where she wasn't by my side, and even now, the ache of that separation remains a reminder of how deeply I cherish her. Samantha, being the first child, always seemed like my parents' favorite, especially my mother's, as she rarely got in trouble or received any whoopings from my dad; in their eyes, she was the perfect child—quiet, obedient, and never speaking back or expressing her own wants. I was the outgoing child, the one who had many friends and wasn't afraid to speak up. I always made sure to share what was on my mind with my parents—not in a disrespectful way, but in a way I felt was honest and appropriate. In contrast, Samantha and I were like day and night. She was quiet, reserved, and rarely voiced her own needs or opinions, while I was more expressive, unafraid to stand up for myself or say what I felt. Our personalities couldn't have been more different, yet those differences made our bond unique, balancing each other out in ways only siblings can. I always felt a deep need to protect Samantha. In elementary school, I found myself in countless fights, standing up for her because others would make fun of her—whether it was about the way she looked, spoke, or acted. Their teasing would ignite a fire in me, and before I knew it, I'd be in a physical fight, regardless of whether it was a boy or a girl. It didn't matter to me who it was—if you messed with my sister, you'd have to deal with me. I couldn't stand to see her hurt, and I would do whatever it took to defend her, even if it meant putting myself in the line of fire. For me, protecting her wasn't just an instinct; it was a responsibility I took to heart.

When I found out Samantha was pregnant by a young man she met while going to work, I was in complete shock. No way—not Samantha. She was always the quiet, reserved one, the sister who seemed too perfect to even notice boys, let alone get involved with one. I had always thought of her as untouchable, the one who never stepped out of line or broke any rules. The news hit me hard, and all I could think about was how our parents would react. What would they think? What would they say? It felt like an unimaginable moment for someone I had always seen as the epitome of innocence and perfection. When the news broke, my parents were furious, especially my father. His anger was palpable, a mix of disappointment and frustration that filled the entire house. He couldn't believe that Samantha—the quiet, obedient daughter he had always trusted—could end up in such a situation. His words were sharp, laced with disbelief and judgment, and the tension was unbearable. My mother, though upset, seemed caught between her own emotions, trying to process the shock while bracing herself for what was to come. It was a moment of chaos where anger, confusion, and hurt collided, leaving a lasting impact on all of us.

My parents wanted nothing to do with the young man who got Samantha pregnant. They refused to meet him, their anger and disappointment too overwhelming to consider opening the door to him. To them, he represented a mistake, a disruption to the image they had of Samantha as their perfect, obedient daughter. Whether it was out of pride, frustration, or simply the hurt of seeing their expectations shattered, they chose to distance themselves from him entirely, making it clear that he was not welcome in their lives or their home. Their refusal only deepened the tension and left Samantha to navigate the situation on her own. The weight of the situation became too much for Samantha to bear, and in her frustration and despair, she began to feel like there was no way out. The shame, the anger from our parents, and the overwhelming emotions surrounding her pregnancy pushed her into a dark place. She felt trapped, isolated, and deeply misunderstood, as though she had let everyone down and there was no path forward. It broke my heart to see her in that state, carrying so much pain that she believed ending her life was the only escape. Her frustration consumed her, and in those moments, it was clear she was crying out for help, for understanding, and for relief from the unbearable weight she was carrying. Overwhelmed by my parents' reaction and the pressure of her situation, Samantha ended up in a mental health facility for a few days. It was her way of escaping the constant judgment, anger, and emotional turmoil that had consumed our home.

She needed space—a break from the relentless weight of disappointment and expectations placed on her. In those days away, I hoped she could find some sense of peace and clarity, far from the chaos that had pushed her to the brink. It was heartbreaking to see her reach such a point, but it was also a reminder of how much she was struggling to cope with everything happening around her. I always knew Samantha was strong, and despite everything she had been through, she found the strength to pull through. After leaving the mental health facility, she made the bold decision to take control of her life. She left home and moved to Connecticut with the young man she was pregnant by, determined to start fresh and build a life for herself and her unborn child. It was a difficult step, but it showed her resilience and her will to rise above the judgment and pressure she had faced. In that moment, she proved that even in the face of hardship, she had the courage to move forward and carve out her own path. When Samantha moved away, a deep sadness settled over me. She wasn't just my sister; she was my closest companion, my confidante, the one I had always counted on to be there. Watching her leave felt like a piece of my heart was being torn away. I understood why she had to go and admired her courage, but it didn't make the pain of her absence any easier to bear. The thought of her being so far away, starting a new chapter of her life without me by her side, left me feeling lonely and empty. It was as if a part of my world had shifted, and I couldn't help but miss her deeply every single day. The first week of her absence was unbearable. I cried every night, unable to sleep, as the weight of her leaving pressed heavily on my heart. The house felt empty without her, and the silence was a constant reminder that she was no longer there. I couldn't bring myself to eat, as the sadness consumed me and took away any sense of normalcy. It felt as though a part of me was missing, and I struggled to adjust to a life without her by my side. The pain of her absence was overwhelming, and I couldn't help but long for the days when we were inseparable.

After that first week, my sadness turned into anger toward Samantha. I couldn't understand how someone I saw and spoke to every single day could suddenly be gone from my life. The closeness we shared felt like it had been ripped away, and the pain of her absence became too much for me to process. I couldn't bring myself to talk to her, and the distance between us grew—not just physically but emotionally too. It was hard on me, on my soul, to go from having her as such a constant part of my life to feeling like she was a stranger in a faraway place. The anger was my way of coping, but deep down, it only masked the hurt I felt from losing her presence in my daily life. After the anger subsided, I slowly began to accept it. I realized that Samantha had made a choice for herself, one she felt was necessary for her own life and future. While the pain of her absence was still there, I started to understand that holding onto my anger would only create more distance between us. Acceptance didn't come easily—it took time and reflection—but eventually, I began to find peace with her decision. Though things weren't the same, I reminded myself of the love we shared and the bond that no amount of distance could truly break. Accepting her absence allowed me to begin healing and holding onto hope that we would reconnect in time. I hadn't spoken to Samantha in months, and the silence between us had grown heavy. Then, one day, there was a knock at the door, and when I opened it, there she was—standing right in front of me.

In that moment, my heart dropped to my chest, overwhelmed by a rush of emotions I couldn't control. I was stunned, unable to speak, as everything I had been holding inside—the hurt, the anger, the longing—came flooding back all at once. Seeing her there felt surreal, like a piece of my life I thought I'd lost had suddenly returned. My heart ached, yet it was also filled with relief and love in a way I couldn't fully explain. It was as if time stood still, and for a moment, everything else disappeared.

Samantha couldn't stay away from her family—she missed us too much. Despite the challenges and everything that had happened, her heart led her back to us. She had left when she was just a few weeks pregnant, but now she returned with a full belly, ready to give birth to her baby girl. Seeing her like that, so close to becoming a mother, was surreal. It felt as though life had come full circle, and even though so much had changed, having her back brought a sense of comfort and wholeness to our family again. It was a bittersweet moment, filled with love, understanding, and the reminder that no matter how far she went, we were always her home.

I remember my parents wanted Samantha to abort the baby. They were consumed with worry about what people would say, how the church would judge her, and how this would ruin her future. To them, the idea of her becoming a young, unmarried mother seemed like the end of everything they had envisioned for her. But Samantha stood her ground. She refused to let their fears dictate her choice, saying with unwavering conviction that she would give birth to her baby. It was a moment that showed her strength and determination, proving that despite the pressure and judgment she faced, she was ready to take responsibility for her child and embrace motherhood on her own terms. It wasn't easy for her, but her courage in that moment was undeniable. Samantha eventually married the young man who fathered her child before moving back home to Florida. While it seemed like the natural next step at the time, I couldn't help but wonder if it was truly the best choice for her life and future. Marriage is a big commitment, and knowing everything she had already been through, I worried whether this relationship would give her the love, stability, and happiness she deserved. It felt like a decision made out of circumstance rather than one rooted in a deep, lasting connection. Even as she moved forward, part of me questioned if she was sacrificing her potential for something that might not fully align with the life I had always dreamed she would have.

On December 8th, 1999, Samantha gave birth to a beautiful, healthy baby girl, and it was the best day of my life. The moment I laid eyes on her, I was overwhelmed with love and joy. She was perfect in every way—her tiny fingers, her soft skin, and the way she looked so peaceful in her little blanket. In that instant, I became an aunt for the first time, and it felt like my heart had grown in ways I never imagined. Seeing Samantha hold her baby, I felt an immense sense of pride and gratitude, knowing this precious child had come into our lives to bring us closer together. It was a day I'll never forget, a day that filled me with hope and a love I never knew I could feel. The young man who fathered my sister's baby had a difficult life of his own. He came from a background filled with challenges, and he didn't have a career or a steady job to provide the stability my sister and the baby needed. His lack of resources and direction made it hard for him to fully step into the role of a provider and partner, leaving my sister to shoulder much of the responsibility on her own. While he may have tried in his own way, the struggles he faced made it clear that he wasn't fully equipped to support a family, which only added to the challenges my sister had to navigate.

Over time, my sister had three more children with the young man, bringing to the world a total of four. Life became increasingly difficult for her as the demands of raising a growing family took their toll. Eventually, their relationship couldn't withstand the pressure, and she divorced him, leaving her to raise the children on her own. It was an incredibly hard journey for her, both financially and spiritually. She struggled to make ends meet, working tirelessly to provide for her kids while trying to maintain her own sense of faith and strength. The weight of being a single mother to four children was overwhelming at times, but she persevered, doing everything in her power to ensure they had what they needed. Her resilience was inspiring, even in the face of such immense challenges.

Over the years, my sister and I grew further apart, barely speaking to one another. What was once a bond so strong and unbreakable turned into distant, sporadic conversations, sometimes only once every couple of months. It was heartbreaking to see someone I had loved so deeply, someone who had been such a huge part of my life, feel like a total stranger. The connection we once shared, the memories we had built together, seemed so far away, replaced by silence and distance. It's a painful feeling to lose that closeness with someone you hold so dear, like a part of your heart has been left behind. Despite the distance between us, I've always held onto the hope that my relationship with Samantha will be restored someday. I'm not sure how or when, but deep down, I believe it's possible. I hope for a time when we can reconnect, heal old wounds, and find our way back to the bond we once shared. No matter how far apart we've drifted, the love I have for her has never gone away, and I carry the hope that one day, we'll rebuild what feels lost. It's a hope I refuse to let go of because I believe our connection is worth saving.

Sometimes, I wonder what Samantha's life would have been like if she had chosen to have an abortion. Would things have been different for her? Would she have avoided the struggles she faced—raising four children on her own and enduring financial and emotional hardship? I think about whether her life would have taken a completely different path, one where she might have pursued the dreams our parents had for her and become something extraordinary. Maybe she could have achieved a life filled with success and stability, free from the burdens that held her back. It's a question I can never truly answer, but it lingers in my mind as I reflect on the sacrifices she made and the challenges she endured because of the choices she stood by so firmly.

I also wonder how different Samantha's life could have been if she had chosen a path guided by her own dreams instead of the expectations of others. She once spoke about becoming a nurse, a dream that seemed so perfectly suited to her caring nature and quiet strength. I can easily imagine her thriving in a hospital, comforting patients with the same gentle spirit she showed at home. But life, with its burdens of family duty and the pressure to please, may have kept her from fully embracing that aspiration.

I know that every decision we make, no matter how small, has the potential to shape our future. Good choices can open doors, create opportunities, and lead to growth, while poor choices can bring challenges or setbacks. For example, choosing to pursue an education, a healthier lifestyle, or kindness toward others often brings long-term rewards—personal fulfillment, stronger relationships, or success. On the other hand, impulsive or short-sighted decisions, like neglecting responsibilities or giving in to harmful habits, can lead to regret, missed opportunities, or struggles. Yet, what's truly powerful is our ability to learn from both good and bad choices. Even mistakes teach us valuable lessons, offering us the chance to grow and make better decisions in the future. In this way, every choice matters, and every path we take helps us become who we are meant to be.

My history with Samantha, my sister, the regret and hopes I had for her, and the pain we experienced together and apart were moments that truly shaped my life and relationship with my family. My sister was not the only sibling with whom I had a turbulent relationship. Just as with Samantha, I had many experiences with my brothers that also taught me numerous life lessons.

My Brother Kalvin & James

Sometimes, the feeling of guilt overwhelms me when I think about not having the chance to say goodbye to my brothers. It's a mix of regret and sadness that tugs at my heart, reminding me of the moments we lost and the words left unspoken. I can't help but wonder if they knew how much I loved them, how much their presence meant to me, and how different life might have been if I'd been able to say that final farewell. At times, it feels like an unfinished chapter in my life, a lingering ache that surfaces whenever I think of them. Yet, in the midst of this guilt, I also hold onto the memories we shared, believing that love can transcend goodbyes and that, somehow, they knew all the things I wish I'd been able to say.

I remember leaving for college while Kalvin and James were still just little boys, and it tore me apart inside. On the one hand, I was excited about the new chapter in my life—the chance to grow, learn, and experience independence—but on the other, I couldn't shake the guilt of walking away from my younger brothers, who still needed guidance and a big sister's presence. I worried about whether they would miss me or if they would resent me for leaving them behind. I was afraid they wouldn't understand that I was doing what I believed was best for my future. Even as I packed my bags and boarded that bus or plane, I could still see their innocent faces in my mind, and I knew I was leaving a piece of my heart at home with them. It's a decision that weighed heavily on me, but it also taught me how sacrifices are sometimes necessary for personal growth and yet, the love for family remains the one constant that never fades.

It was three in the morning when Alex called, telling me he thought James had been shot and might be dead. In that instant, it felt like the ground opened beneath my feet. My heart pounded so loudly I could hardly hear him, and a wave of disbelief and dread rushed through my entire body. My mind raced, trying to grasp what was happening: Could this be real, or was it some horrendous mistake? Fear gripped me so tightly that it felt impossible to breathe, and every second seemed to stretch out like an eternity. I was flooded with questions, panic, and a desperate hope that somehow this was all just a misunderstanding. The rest of that night was a blur of phone calls, tears, and a suffocating sense of helplessness that I couldn't shake, no matter how hard I tried. James shared many of my father's traits his strong will, his stubbornness, and even his habit of keeping emotions locked away—but ironically, those similarities often kept them from having a close relationship. They would butt heads over the smallest things, each one convinced they were right, and neither was eager to back down. Their arguments could escalate quickly, fueled by the very intensity they both carried. Instead of bonding over their shared personalities, they seemed to clash, as if they were mirrors reflecting each other's flaws. In many ways, the qualities that made James so much like my father were the same ones that created distance between them, preventing them from finding common ground or truly understanding one another.

I could tell James needed a father figure in his life—someone who would guide him, nurture him, and show him a sense of acceptance. Even though he tried to act tough and self-reliant, I often saw glimpses of vulnerability beneath that surface. He craved a steady presence to turn to when he felt uncertain or overwhelmed, a warm embrace to reassure him that he mattered. In our household, strong personalities clashed more often than they connected, and James's need for a gentle hand on his shoulder went unmet. He never stopped hoping for that deeper bond, and when it didn't come, it left a lingering void that he tried to fill on his own. It was heartbreaking to watch him strive for independence while still clearly yearning for the kind of fatherly love and guidance that only a caring, supportive dad could provide.

James had a wonderful relationship with our mother—she was the nurturing presence he desperately needed, especially given the tension in our household. Unlike our father's strict discipline, my mom offered James warmth, understanding, and a gentle ear whenever he needed to talk. He would open up to her more than anyone else, and I could see how her patience and kindness provided him with a sense of stability he didn't get from our father. Despite her own challenges and the stress she endured, she always tried to be there for James, giving him the kind of reassurance and emotional support that helped balance out the harsher realities of our home life. Their bond was clear in the quiet moments—like when she'd sit beside him, listening to his worries or celebrating his small victories. While no relationship is without its difficulties, the connection James shared with my mom was a bright spot, something that often kept him grounded when everything else felt uncertain.

James was in and out of jail for much of his young adulthood, which put a tremendous strain on both him and our family. Every time he got out, he spoke about turning his life around, yet he always seemed to slip back into old habits or find himself in the wrong place at the wrong time. It was heartbreaking to watch him struggle with the same pitfalls and face the consequences of poor choices, knowing how much potential he had if only he could break free from the cycle. Despite his tough exterior, I could sense the fear and regret just beneath the surface. Each arrest was a blow to his spirit, but it also tested the resolve and patience of those who loved him. We tried our best to believe in his promises, holding onto hope that one day he'd find a way to stay on the right path.

That wasn't the case, though, because James's life took a tragic turn when he was shot and killed. News of his death was like a punch in the gut, a final blow none of us were ready for. I couldn't stop replaying the moment I received the call, the way my heart seemed to freeze in my chest. It felt surreal—like something you'd see in a movie, not a reality that would crash into your own life. No matter how much trouble James had been in before or how often he'd stumbled along the way, part of me always held onto the hope that he'd turn things around, that he'd find a path out of the chaos. But the gunfire ended every possibility for a second chance. In the days and weeks that followed, I struggled to accept that I wouldn't hear his voice again or see him walk through the door. I was left with questions I could never ask and a yearning for the kind of closure we'd never have. His death was a stark reminder of how fragile and unpredictable life can be, and it haunted me, knowing we all lost the opportunity to witness the man James could've become if he'd only had a little more time.

James left behind a little girl, and it breaks my heart to think about the relationship they might have shared if he had lived. I can only imagine how he would have doted on her—perhaps teaching her new things, cheering her on in school, or simply being there to listen when life got tough. She would have had a father to protect her, guide her, and fill her world with the kind of laughter only a parent can provide. And I can only imagine the depth of my mother's pain when James passed, how the sorrow must have hit her like a crushing wave she never saw coming. She had already endured so much in life, but losing a child is an agony beyond words. I can picture her sitting there, consumed by grief, trying to make sense of a world that had suddenly become darker and emptier. Every memory she had of James—his laughter, his rebellious spirit, the moments when he would confide in her—likely replayed over and over in her mind, each one a bittersweet reminder of the son she could no longer hold. Mothers are supposed to protect their children, to keep them safe from harm, and I know she carried the weight of that unfulfilled promise in her heart. Even as she tried to be strong for the rest of us, the ache of James's absence must have been immeasurable, a wound no amount of time or understanding could fully heal. Nobody was as heartbroken over James's death as my other brother, Kalvin.

Kalvin was born when I was 19 years old, and I was instantly thrilled about having another little brother. The moment my mother brought him home, I fell in love with him. However, I later learned that his conception was a surprise and that my parents, overwhelmed by their responsibilities, were not initially happy—there was even talk of my mother considering an abortion. Despite this turbulent beginning, Kalvin's presence as a baby brought us immense joy. By the time Kalvin turned six, his behavior in school took a troubling turn, coinciding with the period when my sister and I were entering high school. Often, he would return to an empty home because both of our parents were at work, and I suspect he felt neglected. There was also a time when my mother traveled to Haiti for nearly nine months, leaving Kalvin without the nurturing presence he desperately needed. Looking back, it seems that these early experiences robbed him of the consistent love and attention every child deserves, leaving him feeling isolated and misunderstood. In such circumstances, children often express their hurt and confusion through misbehavior, testing boundaries in hopes of getting the attention and reassurance they crave. Over time, the absence of a stable, loving presence in his life likely led Kalvin to seek validation through his actions, ultimately manifesting in the behavioral problems we witnessed.

As Kalvin got older, his behavior spiraled further out of control, and he found himself drawn to the wrong crowd in search of acceptance. What began as minor infractions quickly escalated, and it seemed as though he could hardly go a month without landing back in jail. The pattern of getting released and then returning to the same destructive environment became a vicious cycle that he found difficult to break. Each time he came home, hopes for a fresh start were overshadowed by the pull of negative influences, leaving him more alienated from the family and the love he desperately needed. This turbulent period was marked by constant worry and heartbreak for those who cared about him as they watched Kalvin drift further from the path they had once imagined for him. Kalvin was a troubled soul, forever searching for deliverance from the patterns he could not seem to escape. To everyone who knew him, he possessed a beautiful heart—just a young man who had lost his way—and I loved him with every beat of my own.

He was tall, handsome, and carried a disarming smile, qualities I would remind him of often. Whenever he called needing money, I was there, just as he was there to tell me how much he loved and respected me. He dreamed of one day finding a partner as strong and resilient as I was, but no matter how many times I urged him to choose integrity or drew him toward church, the pull of a darker life was too great. Even news of his becoming a father and the hope that he would serve as an example for his nieces and nephews was not enough to break the cycle of arrests and heartache. He promised me on more than one occasion that each stint in jail would be his last, and I believed him because I wanted so badly for it to be true. One morning, fresh out of jail, he called to say he loved me, a gesture that meant everything. But later that same day, he found himself in the wrong place at the wrong time. He was shot and killed, and in that moment, an entire world of possibilities for him vanished, leaving those of us who cherished him with an ache that words can never fully heal.

Only two months had passed since we buried my brother James, and before I could even begin to process that immense grief, life dealt another devastating blow. When I received the news of Kalvin's death, it felt as if my entire world slammed to a halt. My lungs seemed to forget how to breathe, and every muscle in my body went rigid in disbelief. My cries tore through me, raw and uncontainable, as if releasing them was the only way to confirm I was still alive. Time blurred, and I felt trapped in that singular moment of anguish—powerless, shattered, and unable to grasp how I could possibly endure another loss so soon.

In the midst of my own heartbreak, my thoughts instantly turned to my mother and how this tragedy would weigh upon her. I knew that her pain would be immeasurable, having already lost one child so recently. The image of her collapsing under yet another burden of sorrow haunted me, and I worried that this wound might never heal. Even in the depths of my own despair, I felt a pull to protect her, to shield her from the devastating reality we both had to confront. It was as if my grief and hers were inextricably bound, each amplifying the other, and I yearned to find some way—any way—to ease her suffering. When I broke the news to my mother, she took a deep breath—almost as though she were bracing for an impact that could shatter her completely. In her eyes, I saw every hope she had for Kalvin crumble in an instant; it was as if a part of her had died along with him. There was a stunned, hollow look on her face, a silent grief deeper than words could express. Although she fought to appear strong in that moment, the weight of another unimaginable loss was more than anyone could bear. It was clear that her heart was breaking all over again, and in the quiet between her labored breaths, I could practically hear the fragments of her soul crying out in pain.

Another funeral we had to attend—another agonizing goodbye—and with it, a torrent of questions and anger I couldn't suppress. I felt as though my family might be cursed, overwhelmed by heartbreak after heartbreak. In desperation, I turned to prayer, pleading with God to guide us through the unthinkable. When we laid Kalvin to rest and said our final farewells, I could barely comprehend how quickly and tragically life had changed. Despite my lingering fury and confusion, I tried to find solace in faith, holding on to the fragile hope that we would somehow find the strength to keep going.

Sometimes, I can't help but wonder if there was anything more I could have done to save my brothers—if one small act or different choice could have changed the course of their lives. I've asked myself over and over whether I am somehow meant to be the one who carries our family's story, the one who rises above our pain to heal the generational wounds we've inherited. In my darkest moments, I question why I was born into this family at all, recalling the idea that souls choose their parents and asking why I would choose this path. Yet, when I look at how far I've come—purchasing multiple homes, acquiring assets, and creating a life that breaks the cycle—I feel like I am on the right path and am achieving my purpose. Perhaps I am the one who holds the key to ending the patterns that have haunted us, to shedding light where there was once only darkness. In those moments of self-reflection, I search for what makes me special, and I begin to believe that it may not be a single trait but rather the unrelenting hope and resilience that keep me moving forward, no matter the obstacles.

Loss is Difficult

Loss is an inevitable part of life, whether it comes through the heartbreaking end of a relationship or the profound grief of death. When someone who once filled our daily lives and provided us with comfort and companionship is no longer there, it can feel as if a piece of our identity has been taken away. We may struggle with a sudden emptiness in routines that were once shared, and the emotional pain can surface as anger, sadness, or even numbness. Over time, this deep sense of loss can affect our self-confidence and the way we view the world, shifting our priorities and perspectives. Yet, the experience of grieving and learning to adapt can also foster resilience, teaching us to appreciate life's fleeting moments and to show compassion—not only toward others who are suffering but also toward ourselves as we heal. My biggest fear in life used to be losing the people and things I held dearest—family, friends, a partner, even my job. The thought of it haunted me, and I clung to every relationship and source of security as tightly as I could. Sometimes, the mere possibility of having to live without them was enough to make my heart race and my mind spiral with anxiety. I worried that if I let my guard down, everything I treasured might slip away. Yet, over time, I've learned that fearing loss can be just as painful as the loss itself, robbing me of the chance to savor the moments I do have. It's a lesson that has taken me years and countless tears to understand: that while loss is inevitable, the love, memories, and growth we experience can carry us through and leave us stronger than before.

In the Gospel of Matthew, Jesus frequently addresses fear and how it can undermine our faith and trust in God. For example, in Matthew 6:25–34, He urges us not to worry about everyday needs—like food and clothing—reminding us that God cares for the birds of the air and the lilies of the field and will care for us even more. In Matthew 10:28–31, Jesus teaches that we should not be afraid of those who can harm the body but cannot touch the soul, emphasizing that the Lord knows even the number of hairs on our heads and holds us in profound value. Through these teachings, Jesus reassures us that our fears can be conquered by relying on God's loving care, shifting our focus from anxiety about worldly concerns to faith in a deeper, divine provision. Despite our belief in the words of the Bible and the mercy of our Lord, fear and doubt still creep into our lives because we are human. What is important is that we stay faithful and believe in the power of Jesus.

During my pregnancy with Matthew, I was consumed by an intense fear of losing the child growing inside me. Each twinge or unfamiliar sensation would send my mind racing to the worst possibilities, and every doctor's appointment felt like a fragile checkpoint on a delicate path. I found myself constantly oscillating between excitement and dread, wishing desperately for a healthy baby yet bracing for something to go wrong. Even well-meaning friends and family trying to offer support sometimes caused my anxiety to flare with their stories or advice. Still, in that vulnerable mix of hope and fear, I discovered a depth of love I had never known before—one that propelled me to keep believing in the promise of a new life, no matter how uncertain the journey felt. During that challenging period—and in so many other moments of uncertainty—I found myself leaning heavily on my faith. It was the one constant that steadied my heart when fear threatened to engulf me. Sometimes, I couldn't help but wonder how I would have coped if God hadn't been there as my anchor, offering hope when logic seemed to falter. Even in the midst of anxiety and doubt, turning to prayer and reflection gave me the courage to press on, reminding me that there is a purpose beyond my current circumstances. Without that divine reassurance, I'm not sure how I would have found the strength to move forward, let alone grow stronger in the face of life's many trials.

One thing we must understand is that our time on this earth is finite; sooner or later, we all face the reality that everything here is temporary. Focusing on the fear of loss can consume our energy and overshadow the blessings we currently have. In the Book of Job, we see a powerful illustration of this truth. Job loses his wealth, his children, and even his health—virtually every earthly comfort slips through his fingers. Despite his profound anguish and confusion, he does not abandon his faith in God. His story reminds us that while loss in this life is inevitable, our response and the hope we hold onto can carry us through the darkest moments. Instead of allowing the fear of loss to dictate our lives, we can find strength in trusting that there is meaning beyond our present struggles. Not many of us possess the unwavering faith that Job demonstrated in his trials, yet we can begin to nurture our own faith by starting small and taking it one step at a time. Each day offers moments—both grand and seemingly insignificant—that we can cherish if we remain open-hearted. When we practice gratitude and learn not to take a single breath for granted, we slowly cultivate the resilience to face life's challenges. Even if our faith feels fragile in comparison, every small act of trust, every moment of thankfulness, helps us grow stronger and more grounded in the journey ahead.

I often remind myself that I don't fully know what life has in store, but I do know the God who brought me from Haiti at a young age has a plan far greater than I can imagine. Despite every obstacle and moment of chaos, I believe wholeheartedly in His promise to bless me, my children, and future generations. He is the great "I AM," the One whose power and purpose will stand firm no matter the challenges. In these moments of uncertainty, I lean on the truth of Romans 8:37, knowing that through His love, I am more than a conqueror. Each step I take is guided by divine grace, reminding me that my past does not define my future and that every hardship can lead to a deeper faith, a stronger spirit, and a life that reflects God's abundant blessings.

My Mother and Aunt Bertha

Growing up, my relationship with my mother was fairly stable, yet it was my aunt Bertha who shouldered most of the day-to-day responsibilities of raising us. While my mother would occasionally cook for us, bathe us, wash our hair, or take us to school, it was my aunt who became our constant caregiver and felt like more than a mother figure. Despite this, I have vivid memories of my mother's youthful beauty—her long, silky hair, her radiant skin, and the nightly skincare routine I admired so much that I hoped to emulate it when I became a woman myself. I can't say my mother wasn't good to us; she was there to comfort us and ensure our needs were met. However, her attention was divided, and with my father leaving for the United States just days after I was born, I can only imagine how much she missed him. That longing, along with her own personal challenges, meant that while she offered love and occasional moments of care, it was my aunt who truly filled the role of our hands-on parent.

My mother was one of eight siblings, and she often told me how their father did not acknowledge or support them, forcing their mother to shoulder the burden of providing for the entire family. In a desperate attempt to ensure her children's survival, my grandmother sent some of them—including my mother—to work as domestic servants for other families, where my mother experienced mistreatment and loneliness until her mother managed to bring her home. Poverty weighed heavily on their household, and there were days when my grandmother simply had no food to give. Still, my mother recalls moments of happiness despite the hardships—proof of her resilient spirit. My grandmother, Deborah, was herself a beautiful, tall woman with curly hair who must have carried her own unseen struggles. I often wish I could delve deeper into my grandmother's life—her sorrows, her trials—so I could better understand the circumstances that shaped my mother's upbringing and, ultimately, who she is today.

When my mother left for the United States, she entrusted my aunt Bertha with the task of raising my sister and me. Though I only spoke to my parents once or twice a week, my aunt made certain we were never lacking in care or love. She was a strong woman who had experienced her own share of loss—losing her mother to illness—yet she remained a bright, joyful soul who guided me through childhood with wisdom and tenderness. It was she who taught me to cook, do laundry, and even navigate the world of boys, insisting my sister and I keep ourselves pure until marriage. Her unwavering faith in God inspired us to seek the right path, and to this day, I am grateful for the nights we spent singing Christian songs together, our voices echoing like angels throughout the neighborhood. Because of my aunt, I grew up free from smoking or drinking, and I learned the value of living a life pleasing to God. In many ways, she paved the road for me to become the woman I am today, and I will forever cherish the childhood she worked so hard to provide.

When I arrived in the United States at the age of 15, my mother was doing her best to fill both parental roles. She worked tirelessly as a housekeeper, often returning home completely exhausted. I couldn't help but notice that her relationship with my father was far from perfect; they argued a lot, though I never witnessed any physical altercations. My mother, outspoken and headstrong, would clash with my father's controlling nature, creating a constant tension beneath our roof. Yet, in spite of the fatigue and discord, my mother did everything in her power to provide for us and maintain some semblance of stability in our lives. I could sense the loneliness in my mother, as I never once saw my father bring her flowers or invite her out for a simple dinner. Their routine revolved around home, church, and work, leaving little space for romance or shared affection. I often wondered if she secretly longed for those small gestures of love or if she had simply grown accustomed to a life devoid of them. Even now, I look back on those times with a mixture of sadness and empathy, wishing she could have experienced the warmth and tenderness she truly deserved from my father.

My mother never had the opportunity to learn how to read or write, which made adjusting to the English language especially difficult for her. Without a foundation in literacy, even the simplest tasks—like filling out forms or reading labels—became hurdles she had to overcome every day. I watched her try her best despite these challenges, often relying on others to translate or interpret for her. Yet through it all, she maintained a steadfast resolve, determined to do whatever it took to navigate her new life in the United States. I often overheard my parents arguing about my mother's struggles with reading and writing, and it pained me to see how deeply it affected her. Each time my father raised the subject, she would burst into tears, her sorrow spilling out in quiet sobs that spoke of shame and frustration. I could only imagine the hurt she felt, knowing how hard she tried yet still being met with criticism. It was as if every word exchanged served as a reminder of what she had never been taught, and it weighed heavily on her heart. I often overheard them quarreling about my father's infidelity, their heated accusations and tearful confessions echoing through the walls. Though the details were never made explicit, I could sense the betrayal and heartache my mother felt as she struggled to reconcile her love for him with the pain of his actions. Each argument left her feeling more vulnerable and uncertain, while my father responded in anger or silence, seldom offering the reassurance she desperately needed. It was a heartbreaking cycle that cast a shadow over our home, stirring in me a deep empathy for my mother's suffering.

Even if my father was having an affair, one thing I was certain of was that he would never leave my mother or us, his children. He was present in our lives, but not in the way a father should have been. There was always a distance, an absence that couldn't be ignored. One thing that stood out to me was his annual trips to Haiti—he left every December and never spent Christmas or New Year's with us. It was always my mother, my siblings, and me, filling the void of his absence during what should have been a time of togetherness. I couldn't help but wonder if those trips were more than what he claimed—if perhaps there was another woman or even another family he was going to see. To this day, that question lingers in my mind, a mystery I may never unravel.

Sometimes, I wonder why my mother stayed with my father for so long, enduring the treatment she received from him. Perhaps it was because she had witnessed her own mother endure similar treatment from her father, trapped in what seemed like a painful cycle passed down through generations. Maybe she doubted her own worth, believing she wasn't enough for another man to love her, even though she was young, beautiful, and capable of being with someone who would cherish her. Or perhaps it was the fear of what people or the church might say if she left, the stigma of breaking her family weighing heavily on her heart. She likely held on for the sake of us, her children, wanting to preserve a sense of stability, even as the relationship slowly chipped away at her happiness and spirit. Before I left for college, I could sense that my mother and father's marriage was over, yet they stayed together for the sake of the two boys and my little sister, Alex. Perhaps it was easier for me to say from the outside, but I often wished my mother had found the strength to leave and embrace the life that awaited her. I believed, and still believe, that God had a beautiful purpose and plan for her life—one that didn't require her to endure a broken relationship. If only she could have seen the possibilities beyond the pain, she might have discovered the freedom, joy, and fulfillment that she so deeply deserved.

When I told my mother that I was leaving my boyfriend of five years, she urged me not to leave him, insisting that he was a good young man. But what she didn't seem to understand was that this "good young man" had hit me, slapped me, called me names, and broken my spirit more times than I could count. I couldn't fathom why she would encourage me to stay in such an abusive relationship. Deep down, I knew I deserved better—a man who would love, respect, and cherish me—and this was not that man. My decision to leave infuriated her, and at the time, I felt hurt and confused by her reaction. Now, looking back, I realize that her perspective was shaped by her own experiences. She had endured similar treatment in her relationship with my father but never found the courage to leave. In a way, she was projecting her own fears and pain onto me, unable to see that I was breaking the cycle she herself had been trapped in for so long.

For me, breaking cycles means putting an end to destructive patterns or behaviors that have been repeated over generations. It's recognizing the pain, trauma, or dysfunction passed down within a family or community and making a conscious decision to create a new, healthier path. Breaking cycles often involves self-awareness, courage, and the willingness to confront uncomfortable truths about the past. It means refusing to tolerate what others may have accepted, whether it's abuse, neglect, poverty, or unhealthy relationships. By breaking cycles, we not only free ourselves from the burdens of the past but also pave the way for a better future, ensuring that the next generation isn't bound by the same struggles. It's about healing, growing, and rewriting the narrative for ourselves and those who come after us.

I was determined to break the cycle because I refused to let those destructive patterns be passed down to my son or his future children, should he choose to have any. I wanted him to grow up in an environment that modeled love, respect, and emotional health—a home where he could see the value of healthy relationships and self-worth. I didn't want him to carry the weight of generational pain or feel trapped by the struggles I had witnessed and experienced. By breaking the cycle, I hoped to create a new legacy, one where he could thrive, free from the shadows of the past, and build a future rooted in kindness, understanding, and the confidence to demand the same from the people around him. It wasn't just about changing my own life; it was about transforming the foundation for the generations to come. I know where I come from—I was born into a family that struggled with poverty, and their parents before them faced the same challenges. Generations of hardship and scarcity had shaped our lives, but I was determined not to repeat that pattern. I wanted more for myself and for the generations that would follow. I refused to let where I started define where I would end up. Breaking free from that cycle meant working harder, dreaming bigger, and believing that a different future was possible. I was committed to changing the narrative, not just for myself but for my family, so that poverty would no longer be a defining part of our story.

Now in their late 60s and early 70s, my mother and father are divorced, and my mother has never remarried. I often find myself wondering: what if she had left when she had the chance? When she was still young, beautiful, and full of potential, could she have created a better life for herself and her two boys? Could things have turned out differently for her? I imagine the possibilities—a life filled with more joy, freedom, and fulfillment, unburdened by the struggles she endured in her marriage. While I know she made the choices she thought were best at the time, I can't help but reflect on the strength she could have discovered had she chosen to walk away sooner. It's a bittersweet thought, one that leaves me wishing she had seen the value and worth in herself that I always saw in her.

My father is now alone, battling stage 4 cancer and dementia, and I can't help but wonder how different things might have been if he had made better choices as a father. Would he still be facing this pain and isolation, with none of his children by his side except for me? Instead of holding my mother trapped in a marriage that drained her, what if he had let her go? Perhaps setting her free could have also freed him—allowing him to find healing, remarriage, or even a path toward healthier decisions in his life. It's hard not to think that his choices—the controlling behavior, the infidelity, the lack of emotional connection—might have brought him to the agony he's facing now. While I feel compassion for him, I also see the weight of his decisions reflected in his solitude, and it makes me wonder how differently his story could have unfolded if love, kindness, and humility had shaped his life.

I don't argue with divorce, especially when staying in a relationship or marriage has the potential to destroy your future. If deep down your heart is somewhere else, and the person you're with was never your first choice but only your most convenient choice, it's worth reconsidering. Perhaps you're staying for the sake of the kids or because you're worried about what people will say or think. But the truth is one day, the kids will grow up and leave, and the opinions of others won't matter 20 years from now. What will matter is your happiness, your future, and the choices you make today that will shape your life. Staying in the wrong relationship may rob you of the chance to be with someone truly amazing, someone who aligns with your soul. I believe that, at the end of our lives, we'll be forced to relive the choices we made. When that moment comes, I hope you can look back and be proud of the life you lived—a life built on courage, love, and authenticity.

We all deserve a love that is truly amazing—a love that nurtures our soul, respects our individuality, and inspires us to be the best version of ourselves. It's the kind of love that makes us feel valued, cherished, and understood, where we can be vulnerable without fear and celebrated for who we are. Amazing love isn't perfect, but it's patient, kind, and rooted in mutual respect. It's a love that doesn't just fill a void but brings light, joy, and peace into our lives. No one should settle for less than this because we are all worthy of a love that uplifts us and reminds us of the beauty and potential of our own hearts.

When you look at that person, they make you feel alive in a way that words can't fully capture. It's as though their presence awakens something deep within you—a spark of joy, excitement, and connection. Their smile has the power to light up your world, and in their eyes, you see a reflection of hope, love, and endless possibilities. Being around them doesn't just make you happy; it makes you feel whole as if they were always meant to be part of your story. They don't just exist in your life; they breathe life into it.

A love like that is hard to find; it's rare and extraordinary, the kind that feels almost magical. It's not just about passion or attraction—it's a connection that runs deeper, touching the very core of who you are. This kind of love understands your flaws and embraces them, celebrates your strengths, and grows stronger through life's challenges. It's the kind of love that feels like home, where you can truly be yourself without fear or pretenses. A love like this doesn't come along often, and when it does, it's something to cherish, protect, and hold onto because it's the kind of love that transforms your life in ways you never imagined.

A love that you can't wait to come home to is the kind that brings you peace and joy no matter how chaotic the world may be. It's the love that feels like a warm embrace after a long day, where the simple act of being together makes everything feel right again. It's the excitement of knowing someone is waiting for you, ready to share laughter, stories, or even the quiet moments of just being near. This kind of love makes home more than just a place—it becomes a feeling, a sanctuary, a reminder that you're loved, valued, and never alone. It's the kind of love that makes every return feel like the best part of your day.

When they touch you, it's as if their hands carry more than just warmth—they carry a spark that ignites something deep within you. Their touch has the power to remind you that you're alive, not just existing, but truly feeling every moment. It's not just physical; it's an energy, a connection that goes beyond words, making your heart race and your soul stir. Their touch is comforting yet electrifying, grounding yet exhilarating, and it makes you feel seen, cherished, and whole in a way nothing else can.

It's the kind of love where, after an intense and passionate moment, you find yourself sitting on top of him, catching your breath, and spilling your thoughts without holding back. He listens intently, not just to your words but to the emotions behind them, as if every detail you share matters deeply to him. In those moments, it's not just about the physical connection—it's about the way he makes you feel heard, valued, and understood. His gaze stays locked on you, his touch gentle yet grounding, as if he's silently telling you that this moment, this exchange, is just as meaningful to him as it is to you. It's a love where, even in the quiet aftermath, you feel completely alive and utterly seen.

It is a love you cannot explain, the kind that goes beyond words, beyond logic, and beyond reason. It's a feeling so deep and profound that it defies explanation—something you just know in your soul. It's the way their presence feels like home, how their smile can brighten the darkest day, and how their absence leaves a void that nothing else can fill. It's a connection that transcends the physical, weaving together your hearts in a way that feels destined. It's a love that doesn't need to be understood or defined because it simply is—pure, unshakable, and entirely yours.

If you're fortunate enough to have that kind of love, hold it tight and never let it go. Cherish it, nurture it, and protect it because love like that is rare and precious. It's the kind of connection that can transform your life, bringing light to the darkest moments and joy to the simplest ones. Don't take it for granted—pour your heart into it, express your gratitude, and show your partner just how much they mean to you every single day. True love is a gift, and when you have it, it's worth everything to keep it alive and thriving.

If you haven't found that love yet, I hope you do. I hope you never give up on the possibility of a connection so deep and fulfilling that it changes everything. Somewhere out there, I believe there's a soul that's meant to meet yours—a love that will come into your life when the time is right. It may not happen as quickly as you hope but trust that the journey is preparing you for something extraordinary. Keep your heart open, hold onto hope, and believe that one day, your paths will cross, and you'll understand why the wait was worth it.

If you did find that kind of love and let them go, I know they will always be the one that got away. No matter where life takes you or who you're with later on, their memory will linger—etched in the corners of your mind and tucked away in the quiet moments of your days. They'll live in your thoughts, a bittersweet reminder of what could have been, and even when you're old and gray, their presence will haunt you in a way no one else can. If life gave second chances, if reliving it were possible, I hope you would choose them. I hope you'd hold onto them and never let them slip away, knowing now the weight of their absence and the gift of their love.

I had believed that I had found this kind of love for a while, but proceeding events made me question my choices and consider a difficult decision.

Gendry was unlike anyone I had ever met. Handsome, single, and full of life, he carried himself with an effortless charm that seemed to brighten every room he entered. But it wasn't just his looks or his charisma that made him stand out—it was something deeper. There was a quiet strength about him, a certain calmness that made him easy to trust, yet there was also an air of mystery that hinted at something more beneath the surface. From the moment I got to know him, I could tell Gendry wasn't the type to wear his heart on his sleeve. He was respectful and kind, always going out of his way to make others feel seen and valued. A gentle soul, he had a way of listening that made you feel like the most important person in the world. Yet, behind his warm demeanor, I could sense layers of unspoken emotions—a quiet weight he carried but rarely shared.

I always felt there was more to Gendry than he let on. He was the kind of person who chose his words carefully, never saying too much but always saying enough. It was this quiet restraint that intrigued me, that made me want to understand him more. He seemed to walk through life with a blend of confidence and guardedness, like someone who had been shaped by both love and loss.

One of the first things I noticed about Gendry was his strained relationship with his family. He rarely spoke about them, and when he did, it was clear that there was a disconnect. He had sisters, but they weren't close. I couldn't help but wonder why. When I asked him about it, he shrugged it off with a simple answer: "We're just not close." At first, I didn't push further. I thought perhaps it was just the way his family functioned—a dynamic that didn't prioritize closeness. But as I got to know him better, I began to sense that there was more to the story. His avoidance wasn't just indifference; it felt like self-preservation. It was as though keeping his distance from his sisters was a way of protecting himself from something painful. I couldn't imagine what could cause such a divide. Was it conflict? Misunderstanding? Or simply a lack of connection? Whatever it was, Gendry didn't elaborate, and I respected his boundaries. But it saddened me to see this part of his life remain unresolved, especially because Gendry seemed like someone who had so much love to give. I wondered how it felt for him, to carry that distance, to know his sisters existed but not be able to reach them emotionally. Did it bother him? Or had he grown used to it, burying the pain so deeply that he no longer felt it?

While Gendry's relationship with his sisters was distant, his bond with his grandmother was the complete opposite. She was the first person he introduced me to, and from the moment I met her, I understood why she held such a special place in his life. She radiated warmth and love, the kind of person who made you feel like you belonged, even if you had just met her. Her presence was comforting, like a safe harbor in the middle of a storm. Gendry's face lit up when he talked about her. She wasn't just his grandmother—she was his confidante, his anchor, the person who had been there for him when others hadn't. It was clear that she had played a significant role in shaping the man he had become. Through her, I got a glimpse of Gendry's softer side, the part of him that was deeply loving and loyal. But even as I admired the bond they shared, I couldn't ignore the emotions Gendry seemed to carry with him. There were moments when his eyes would drift off as if he were lost in thought, moments when his laughter seemed tinged with sadness. It was as though being close to his grandmother reminded him of something he had lost or perhaps something he longed for. I didn't know what it was, but I could feel it in the quiet moments, in the pauses between words.

Gendry was the kind of person who didn't talk about his feelings easily. He had a way of redirecting conversations away from himself, focusing instead on others. But even in his silence, I could sense the weight he carried. It was in the way his shoulders sometimes slumped when he thought no one was looking, in the way his smile didn't always reach his eyes. Gendry was carrying something—perhaps pain, regret, or unresolved emotions—but he kept it locked away, hidden behind his calm exterior. I often wondered if his distance from his family played a role in this. Did he feel the absence of those connections? Did he ever wish things were different? Or had he resigned himself to the way things were, convincing himself that some relationships were better left untouched? I didn't know, and I wasn't sure if he wanted me to. But I cared deeply for Gendry, and it hurt to see him burdened by something he wouldn't—or couldn't—share. At the same time, I admired his resilience. Whatever he had been through, it hadn't hardened him. He was still kind, still respectful, still full of life in so many ways. It was a testament to his character, to the strength of his soul. Even when he was struggling internally, he made an effort to bring joy to those around him. That kind of strength is rare, and it made me love him even more.

Being with Gendry was a journey of discovery. I wanted to understand him, to peel back the layers of his complexity, but I also knew that he needed to let me in on his own terms. He wasn't the type to open up easily, and I didn't want to push him. Instead, I tried to create a safe space for him, to let him know that I was there if he ever wanted to share. I also learned to appreciate the beauty in his mystery. Not everything needed to be explained or resolved right away. Sometimes, just being present—just loving him as he was—was enough. Gendry didn't need to have it all figured out, and neither did I. What mattered was that we had each other, that we were building something together, even if parts of his past remained unspoken.

Gendry was, and still is, one of the most complex and beautiful souls I've ever known. He taught me that people are not always what they seem on the surface and that there are stories behind every smile and every silence. His gentle nature, his respect for others, and his love for his grandmother showed me the depth of his heart. At the same time, his strained family relationships and his quiet struggles reminded me that even the strongest people carry wounds. Gendry had a way of carrying himself that drew people in—his charm, his warm smile, and the kindness that radiated from him made him someone everyone wanted to be around. But as I got to know him, I realized that beneath his lighthearted exterior was a man shaped by deep pain and profound loss. The more he opened up to me, the more I came to understand the struggles he carried and the more I admired the quiet strength that allowed him to move forward despite it all.

One day, in a rare moment of vulnerability, Gendry shared a part of his story that broke my heart. He told me about his mother, the woman who should have been his first source of unconditional love and support, but who left him when he was still a young man. She walked away before he even turned 18, at a time when he needed her most. As he spoke, his voice was steady, but I could see the pain lingering in his eyes, the wounds that time hadn't fully healed.

Gendry admitted that his mother's absence had left a mark on him, one that shaped how he saw himself and his relationships. "When your own mother leaves," he said, "it makes you feel like you're not enough for anyone to stay." His words were raw and unfiltered, and they revealed a vulnerability that he rarely allowed to surface. He confessed that he carried a deep fear that everyone he loved would eventually leave him, just as his mother had. Even though he knew intellectually that not everyone would abandon him, the emotional scars from his childhood were hard to ignore. He carried that fear into his relationships, sometimes building walls to protect himself from getting hurt, other times holding back parts of himself because he wasn't sure if he could trust anyone to stay. Hearing Gendry talk about this fear broke my heart. It made me realize how much courage it took for him to let me in, to trust me enough to share this part of his story. It also made me understand the quiet struggles he faced every day—the battle between wanting to love fully and fearing that love would leave him broken.

As we talked more, Gendry opened up about another profound loss in his life: the death of his father. He spoke about his father with such tenderness and love that I could feel the depth of their bond. "He was my hero," Gendry said quietly, his voice tinged with both pride and sorrow. His father had been his rock, the person he looked up to and relied on. Losing him to bone cancer was a pain that Gendry carried every day, even though he rarely talked about it. Gendry described his father as a kind, hardworking man who loved his family deeply. Even as his father battled cancer, he remained a source of strength and inspiration for Gendry. "He never complained, even when the pain was unbearable," Gendry told me. "He just kept going because he didn't want us to worry."

Gendry's admiration for his father was clear, but so was the grief he still carried. Losing someone you love deeply leaves a void that can never truly be filled, and for Gendry, that void was magnified by the fact that his father had been one of the few constants in his life. His mother's absence had already left him feeling abandoned, and losing his father felt like losing his foundation. As Gendry shared these stories with me, I began to see how much his past had shaped him. His mother's departure and his father's death were defining moments that had left lasting scars, but they had also shaped his character in profound ways. Gendry's pain had made him more empathetic and more aware of the struggles others carried. It had also given him a quiet strength that allowed him to keep moving forward, even when life felt overwhelming. One of the things that stood out to me was how much Gendry leaned on his grandmother for support. She had become a second mother to him, stepping in to fill the void left by his mother's absence. Gendry's relationship with her was a source of comfort and stability, and it was clear that she had been instrumental in helping him navigate the challenges he faced.

"She's the one person I know I can count on," Gendry told me. "She's always been there for me, no matter what." His love for his grandmother was evident, and it was a testament to the kind of man he was—loyal, loving, and deeply appreciative of the people who stood by him.

Gendry's experiences with loss and abandonment had a profound impact on his relationships. He wanted to love and be loved, but his fear of losing people often held him back. At times, he would retreat emotionally, keeping people at arm's length to protect himself from potential pain. Other times, he would overcompensate, trying to be everything for everyone in an effort to prove his worth.

Being close to Gendry meant understanding these complexities and being patient with him as he navigated his fears. It wasn't always easy, but it was worth it. Gendry's heart was big, and his capacity for love was immense. He just needed to feel safe enough to let that love flow freely. I did my best to give him comfort, ease his fears, and make him feel loved. Eventually, issues began creeping up in our marriage, which I could not ignore.

The First Red Flag

I asked Gendry early on if he had ever been married, and his answer was clear: "No, I've never been married." I didn't question it. Why would I? He said it with such confidence and ease that I had no reason to doubt him. At that moment, I believed him completely. For a year, our relationship grew. We shared moments of laughter, love, and vulnerability—or so I thought. Gendry had a way of making me feel special like I was the center of his world. I saw a future with him, and I trusted him to be honest with me about who he was and where he had been. But that trust would later be shaken to its core.

It was a year into our relationship when I found out the truth: Gendry had been married before. Twice. I was his third wife. I was blindsided. The revelation hit me like a punch to the stomach, leaving me breathless and reeling. I couldn't believe that someone I cared so deeply for, someone I thought I knew so well, had kept such a significant part of his life hidden from me. I confronted Gendry immediately. The words tumbled out of me—angry, hurt, and desperate for answers. "Why didn't you tell me? Why did you lie?" I demanded, my voice trembling with emotion. I wanted to understand how he could keep something so important from me, how he could look me in the eyes every day and pretend like his past didn't exist. His answer only deepened my confusion. "I lied," he said, "because I knew if I told you, you'd never give me a chance." His voice was steady, almost resigned as if he had accepted this truth long before I had. "You're fresh out of college, never married, and I knew that if you knew about my past, you'd never agree to be with me." His words hung in the air, heavy with the weight of his choices. And in some ways, he wasn't wrong. If Gendry had told me the truth from the beginning, I might not have given him a chance. I was young, idealistic, and looking for someone whose life matched the image I had for my future. The idea of being with someone who had already been through two marriages would have scared me, and he knew that. But knowing that didn't make the betrayal hurt any less.

What hurt most wasn't just the lie—it was the fact that he had made the decision for me. By withholding the truth, Gendry had taken away my ability to choose. He had decided that his desires were more important than my right to make an informed decision about who I wanted to be with. It was a betrayal of trust, one that cut deeper than I could have imagined. Looking back, I can see now that this was the first red flag—the moment I should have walked away. A relationship built on deception can't stand, no matter how strong the feelings are. Gendry's lie wasn't just a mistake; it was a deliberate choice to manipulate the foundation of our relationship. It was a sign that trust, the cornerstone of any partnership, was already broken. And yet, I stayed. Despite my anger, my hurt, and my better judgment, I stayed. I told myself that people make mistakes, that maybe Gendry had lied out of fear rather than malice. I convinced myself that the connection we shared was worth salvaging, that this one lie didn't have to define our future. But deep down, I knew the truth: I stayed because I didn't want to let go of the idea of us. I stayed because I wasn't ready to face the reality of what his lie meant.

The months that followed were a whirlwind of emotions. I tried to move past the betrayal, to rebuild the trust that had been shattered. But the truth lingered like a shadow over our relationship, coloring every interaction with doubt. I found myself questioning everything—his words, his actions, even his love for me. If he could lie about something as significant as his marriage, what else might he be hiding?

At the same time, I was wrestling with my own guilt and uncertainty. Was I being too harsh? Was I holding him to an impossible standard? After all, hadn't he been honest with me eventually? Didn't everyone deserve a second chance? These thoughts swirled in my mind, making it impossible to find clarity. Gendry, for his part, seemed genuinely remorseful. He apologized repeatedly, promising that he would never lie to me again. He opened up about his past, sharing details about his marriages and the reasons they didn't work out. He told me about the pain of those relationships, the lessons he had learned, and his desire to build something better with me. His vulnerability made it harder to walk away. I wanted to believe him. I wanted to believe that his remorse was real and that we could move forward together.

But no matter how much I wanted to believe in us, the cracks in our foundation were impossible to ignore. Trust, once broken, is incredibly hard to rebuild. Every time I looked at Gendry, I couldn't help but wonder: What else isn't he telling me? The doubt gnawed at me, slowly eroding the love and connection we had once shared. In hindsight, I can see that staying was a mistake. I ignored the red flags because I didn't want to face the pain of letting go. I clung to the hope that things could get better, that Gendry could prove himself worthy of the trust he had broken. But the truth is, a relationship built on deception will always be fragile. No matter how much effort we put into repairing the damage, the foundation was too weak to support the weight of our future. When Gendry and I first met, our connection felt immediate and profound. Despite discovering his previous marriages—a truth he had initially concealed—I chose to stay, believing in our love and hoping for future honesty. We married and welcomed our son, Matthew. I embraced the role of a stay-at-home mother, dedicating myself to Matthew's upbringing and managing our household. Gendry worked diligently to provide for us. On the surface, our life seemed idyllic

Over time, subtle cracks appeared in our seemingly perfect life. Gendry's work hours grew longer, and he became increasingly distant. Our once open communication dwindled, replaced by strained and superficial conversations. I sensed an emotional chasm growing between us but struggled to identify its source. My role as a stay-at-home mom, while fulfilling, also became isolating. The daily routine of caring for Matthew and managing the household left little room for personal growth. I began to feel disconnected from the vibrant woman I once was.

Shattered Trust

Then, I found out something that I never imagined, that I always hoped and prayed would not happen to me. I discovered that Gendry was unfaithful and my entire world came crashing down. The man I had trusted, the man I had married, and the father of my child had betrayed me in a way that felt unbearable. It wasn't just one woman—it was multiple women. Each revelation felt like a fresh wound, deepening the pain and leaving me questioning everything I thought I knew about him, about our marriage, and even about myself. At first, I couldn't believe it. I didn't want to believe it. I kept hoping that, somehow, it wasn't true—that there was some explanation that would make it all go away. But the evidence was undeniable, and as the truth sank in, I felt a pain unlike anything I'd ever experienced. It wasn't just the betrayal that hurt; it was the realization that the life I thought we were building together was not what it seemed. Our marriage, the family we had created, was tainted by secrets and lies.

I knew immediately that I couldn't be intimate with Gendry anymore. The thought of being close to him, of letting him touch me, made my stomach turn. Every time I looked at him, I saw his betrayal, and the weight of that hurt was too much to bear. Yet, despite everything, I couldn't bring myself to leave. I didn't want to put Matthew through the pain of a broken family. I told myself I was staying for him, to give him stability and a sense of normalcy. But in doing so, I sacrificed my own sense of peace. Living under the same roof as Gendry, pretending to be a couple for Matthew's sake, was one of the hardest things I've ever done. There were days when I wanted to scream at him, to demand answers, to make him feel the depth of the pain he had caused me. But more often than not, I bottled it up. I went through the motions of daily life—cooking, cleaning, taking care of Matthew—as though everything was fine. On the outside, I played the role of a devoted wife and mother. But on the inside, I was falling apart.

The nights were the hardest. When the house was quiet and Matthew was asleep, I was left alone with my thoughts. The weight of my emotions would hit me like a tidal wave—anger, sadness, betrayal, and a deep sense of loss. I would lie in bed, staring at the ceiling, replaying every moment of our relationship in my mind. I wondered if there were signs I had missed, moments when I should have realized something was wrong. I questioned myself, wondering if I had done something to push him away or if I simply wasn't enough for him. There were nights when the pain was so overwhelming that I couldn't stop the tears from falling. I would cry silently, not wanting Gendry to hear me, not wanting to give him the satisfaction of knowing how deeply he had hurt me. But even in my silence, the pain was palpable. It felt like a weight pressing down on my chest, making it hard to breathe. I felt trapped in a cycle of hurt and anger, unable to move forward but unwilling to let go.

Gendry, for his part, seemed to regret what he had done. He would apologize over and over, telling me how sorry he was and how much he wanted to fix things. He would beg me to give him another chance, to let him prove that he could change. But his words felt hollow to me. How could I trust him again after everything he had done? How could I believe in his promises when he had already broken so many? I refused to let him back into my heart, and I refused to let him back into my bed. I built walls around myself, walls that I thought would protect me from further pain. But those walls also isolated me. While Gendry tried to make amends, I shut him out completely. I didn't want to hear his excuses or his explanations. I didn't want to give him the chance to hurt me again.

For more than a year, we lived together as a couple in name only. To the outside world, we were still a family. We still attended events together and still celebrated birthdays and holidays as though nothing was wrong. But behind closed doors, the cracks in our li relationship were impossible to ignore. We barely spoke, and when we did, it was only about practical matters—Matthew's school, the bills, the schedule for the week. The intimacy and connection that once defined our relationship were gone, replaced by a cold and distant coexistence. I felt like I was living a double life. On the one hand, I was trying to be the best mother I could be for Matthew, giving him love and stability even as my own heart was breaking. On the other hand, I was navigating the pain of a marriage that felt irreparably broken. The weight of it all was exhausting, and there were days when I didn't know how much longer I could keep going.

The emotional toll of staying in the marriage was immense. I felt like I had lost a part of myself—my confidence, my joy, my sense of who I was. I had always thought of myself as a strong and independent woman, but Gendry's betrayal had shaken me to my core. I felt weak and vulnerable, as though the foundation I had built my life on had crumbled beneath me. There were moments when I resented Gendry for what he had done, not just to me but to our family. I resented the choices he had made, the lies he had told, and the pain he had caused. But I also resented myself for staying, for allowing myself to remain in a situation that caused me so much pain. I felt trapped between two equally painful options—staying in a broken marriage or breaking apart the family I had worked so hard to build.

Many would question my decision; they would ask me why I stayed and why I allowed myself to live in such pain for so long.

At the heart of it all was Matthew. I stayed because I wanted to protect him, to shield him from the pain of a broken family. I told myself that as long as he was happy and cared for, I could endure the pain. But deep down, I wondered if I was really doing the right thing. Was I teaching Matthew that it was okay to settle for less than he deserved? Was I modeling a healthy relationship, or was I showing him the cracks in our foundation?

Finding Strength in the Pain

Through all of this, I learned a lot about myself. I learned that pain, no matter how deep, doesn't define me. I learned that I am stronger than I ever thought I could be. And I learned that love—real, honest love—requires trust and respect, neither of which could exist in the aftermath of Gendry's betrayal. Even though I stayed, I began to focus on myself in small ways. I found moments of joy in caring for Matthew, in reconnecting with friends, and in remembering the things that made me feel alive. Slowly but surely, I started to rebuild my sense of self, even as my marriage remained in shambles.

Discovering the World of Influence

I found myself at a crossroads. I had the choice to remain stuck in my pain or to channel my energy into something meaningful, something that could give me purpose and remind me of my worth. It was during this time that I discovered a new path—one that not only transformed my career but also reignited my sense of self-worth and independence.

It began almost by accident. I had always been passionate about skincare and self-care, and I often shared tips and routines with friends and family. One day, I decided to post a simple video on social media about my personal skincare journey. I didn't think much of it at the time—it was just a way to share something I loved. But to my surprise, the video resonated with people. The comments started pouring in, with viewers asking for more tips, product recommendations, and advice. What started as a hobby quickly turned into something bigger. My social media following grew rapidly, and soon, brands began reaching out to collaborate. At first, it was small partnerships—free products in exchange for posts—but as my audience expanded, so did the opportunities. I realized that I had stumbled upon a career that combined my passions, creativity, and entrepreneurial spirit.

Becoming an influencer was more than just sharing content; it was about building a personal brand that people could trust and relate to. I poured my heart into creating high-quality, authentic content that reflected who I was and what I stood for. I didn't just want to be another face on social media—I wanted to make a genuine impact. I spent countless hours learning the ins and outs of content creation, from photography and videography to marketing and analytics. I studied what made certain influencers successful and applied those lessons to my own strategy. I also made it a point to stay true to myself, only partnering with brands that aligned with my values and resonated with my audience.

As my platform grew, I began working with major brands in the beauty, wellness, and fashion industries. These partnerships not only validated my hard work but also opened doors to opportunities I had never imagined. I became a voice in the industry, someone people looked to for inspiration and guidance.

My success as an influencer eventually inspired me to take things a step further. Skincare had always been a passion of mine, and I often dreamed of creating my own products—ones that were effective, affordable, and rooted in clean, sustainable practices. With the support of my growing platform, I decided to turn that dream into reality. Launching a skincare line was no small feat. It required months of research, testing, and development. I worked closely with chemists and industry experts to create formulas that met my high standards. I wanted every product to reflect my commitment to quality and authenticity, and I refused to cut corners. The day my skincare line launched was one of the proudest moments of my life. Seeing my vision come to life, holding the products in my hands, and hearing the positive feedback from customers was incredibly rewarding. It was a testament to the hard work, resilience, and passion I had poured into the project.

As my influence and experience in the industry grew, I realized there was another avenue where I could make an impact. Many of the brands I worked with struggled with their digital presence and marketing strategies. I saw an opportunity to help them not just as an influencer but as a partner who could guide them in navigating the digital landscape. I decided to launch my own digital marketing company, leveraging the skills I had developed as an influencer. I understood the power of storytelling, branding, and social media, and I wanted to use that knowledge to help businesses thrive. My company focused on providing personalized marketing strategies, social media management, and content creation services tailored to each client's needs.

Starting the company was both exciting and challenging. I had to learn how to manage a team, handle logistics, and balance multiple projects at once. But it was also incredibly fulfilling to see my clients succeed, knowing that I had played a part in their growth.

Through it all, my work became a source of strength and healing. It gave me a sense of purpose during a time when my personal life felt uncertain. It reminded me of my resilience and capability, showing me that I could build something meaningful despite the challenges I faced. My journey as an influencer, entrepreneur, and business owner also allowed me to redefine my identity. I was no longer just a wife or a mother—I was a successful, independent woman carving out her own path. I found joy in the process of creating, connecting, and building, and it gave me the confidence to face the difficulties in my marriage with a renewed sense of clarity.

While my career was flourishing, I remained deeply committed to my role as a mother. Matthew was always my priority, and I worked hard to ensure that he felt loved, supported, and cared for. Balancing work and family wasn't always easy, but I learned to manage my time effectively, carving out moments to be fully present with him while also pursuing my professional goals. In many ways, my success was for Matthew. I wanted to show him that strength, determination, and passion could overcome even the most difficult circumstances. I wanted him to see that his mother was capable of building something extraordinary, not just for herself but for our family.

My journey from a betrayed wife to a successful entrepreneur is one of resilience, transformation, and empowerment. What began as a painful chapter in my life ultimately became the catalyst for growth and success. I turned my pain into purpose, using it as fuel to build a career that not only fulfilled me but also inspired others. Today, as I reflect on how far I've come, I'm reminded of the power of perseverance. I'm grateful for the challenges that pushed me to discover my potential and for the opportunities that allowed me to thrive. My journey is far from over, but I face the future with hope, confidence, and a sense of purpose that comes from knowing who I am and what I'm capable of achieving.

The Reflection Within: Why Did I Attract This?

In the quiet moments after my marriage ended, I found myself consumed by one lingering question: What is it in me that drew me to someone who couldn't love me the way I deserved? It wasn't just about Gendry anymore—it was about me, about the patterns that seemed to repeat themselves, about the choices I made, and the love I accepted. As painful as it was to look inward, I knew I couldn't move forward without first understanding myself. I began to question everything. I replayed the moments in my relationship with Gendry over and over in my mind, dissecting every interaction, every red flag I ignored, every time I convinced myself that things would get better. I asked myself why I had stayed for so long, even when I knew deep down that I wasn't happy. Why did I tolerate the lies, the betrayal, and the distance? Why did I keep hoping that Gendry would change, even when his actions told me otherwise? The answers didn't come easily. I had to sit with uncomfortable truths about myself—truths I had avoided for years. I realized that while Gendry's behavior was his responsibility, my acceptance of it said something about me. It forced me to confront the parts of myself that I had neglected, the wounds I had carried for so long that I didn't even realize they were there.

One of the hardest realizations was that, deep down, I didn't value myself as much as I thought I did. I had spent so much of my life prioritizing others—making sure they were happy, cared for, and loved—that I rarely stopped to ask if I was receiving the same in return. I had equated love with sacrifice, believing that if I gave enough, if I worked hard enough, I could earn the love I desired. But love isn't something that should have to be earned. True love is freely given, built on mutual respect and trust. In my relationship with Gendry, I had settled for less than I deserved because I didn't fully believe I was worthy of more. I had accepted his excuses, forgiven his betrayals, and ignored the warning signs because I was afraid—afraid of being alone, afraid of starting over, and afraid of admitting that my marriage wasn't what I wanted it to be.

As I dug deeper, I began to see patterns that went back further than Gendry. I saw how my upbringing, my past relationships, and even societal expectations had shaped the way I viewed myself and love. I realized that I had always been a giver, someone who found purpose in meeting the needs of others. While this was a beautiful trait, it often came at the expense of my own needs and boundaries. I thought about the messages I had internalized over the years—that being a good wife meant enduring, that love required compromise, that my worth was tied to how much I could give to others. These beliefs had led me to tolerate relationships that were one-sided, where my emotional well-being took a backseat to someone else's comfort. Gendry was just one example of a larger pattern in my life, and acknowledging that was both painful and liberating.

Once I recognized these patterns, I began to ask myself some of the hardest questions I've ever faced: Why did I believe I wasn't enough? Why did I feel the need to prove my worth through sacrifice? What was it in me that made me stay in relationships where I wasn't valued? The answers weren't always clear, but they pointed to a common theme: I had spent so much time looking for love and validation outside of myself that I hadn't learned how to give it to myself. I was seeking from others what I needed to find within—self-worth, self-respect, and self-love.

As difficult as it was to face these truths, they also gave me a sense of direction. If I wanted to attract a love that was healthy, honest, and fulfilling, I had to start by changing the way I loved myself. I had to learn how to set boundaries, how to communicate my needs, and how to walk away from relationships that didn't honor who I was. I realized that I couldn't expect someone else to value me if I didn't value myself. I couldn't expect someone else to respect my boundaries if I wasn't willing to enforce them. And I couldn't expect someone else to love me unconditionally if I didn't learn how to love myself first.

The journey of healing wasn't easy. It required me to confront parts of myself that I had buried for years. I had to unlearn the belief that my worth was tied to how much I could give to others. I had to challenge the narrative that being alone was something to fear. And I had to let go of the idea that love was something I had to earn. I began to focus on myself in ways I never had before. I explored my passions, reconnected with my values, and surrounded myself with people who uplifted me. I learned to celebrate my own accomplishments, to speak kindly to myself, and to prioritize my own well-being. Slowly but surely, I began to rebuild the relationship I had with myself.

As I grew stronger, I began to see myself in a new light. I realized that I was enough—not because of what I could do for others, but simply because of who I was. I didn't need someone else to complete me or validate me. I was whole on my own, and that realization was incredibly empowering. I also came to understand that my past didn't define me. While Gendry's actions had caused me pain, they didn't determine my future. I had the power to break free from old patterns, to choose a different path, and to create a life filled with the kind of love and respect I deserved.

Today, I carry the lessons of my past with me, not as burdens, but as reminders of how far I've come. I no longer question my worth or settle for less than I deserve. I know that love begins with self-respect and that the right person will honor me for who I am, not for what I can give. The journey to understanding myself has been one of the hardest, but also one of the most rewarding. It has taught me that the most important relationship I'll ever have is the one I have with myself. And it has shown me that when I value and love myself, I attract relationships that reflect that same energy. This process has been about more than just healing from Gendry—it's been about rediscovering who I am, what I want, and what I deserve. And for that, I'm deeply grateful.

One I realized just how much I was really worth, I knew what had to be done. I had to divorce Gendry.

Matthew's Well-Being: My Greatest Concern

When I made the decision to divorce Gendry, my biggest concern wasn't about myself or even Gendry—it was about Matthew. I knew that growing up in a divorced family would come with its own set of challenges, and the thought of him not receiving love from both of his parents weighed heavily on my heart. As his mother, I wanted to protect him from pain, shield him from the emotional scars of our broken marriage, and ensure that he still felt secure and loved.

But I also knew the reality: a household filled with tension, mistrust, and unhappiness wasn't the kind of environment I wanted Matthew to grow up in. Staying together for his sake wasn't truly for his sake—it was prolonging a situation that wasn't healthy for anyone involved. If anything, I realized that it was better for Matthew to grow up in a home where at least one parent was happy, fulfilled, and emotionally stable. I had to believe that my decision to leave was ultimately the best thing for him, even if it wasn't easy in the short term.

Once the drivorce process was complete, I worked very had to make sure that Matthew was as happy and cared for as possible. I wanted him to have the love of both his parents. Despite my pain and anger toward Gendry, I knew that I couldn't let those feelings dictate how we co-parented. Matthew needed both of us in his life, and it was my responsibility to create a space where that could happen. I couldn't allow my hurt to spill over into my relationship with Gendry when it came to Matthew. For his sake, I had to find a way to forgive, or at least to let go of the bitterness enough to work together as parents.

The idea of co-parenting with someone who had caused me so much pain felt impossible at first. How could I speak to Gendry with kindness when I still felt the sting of his betrayal? How could I trust him to be a good father to Matthew when he had failed me as a husband? These questions kept me awake at night, but I knew I didn't have the luxury of avoiding them. Matthew's well-being depended on us finding a way to make it work.

In my darkest moments, when the weight of it all felt unbearable, I turned to God for guidance. I prayed for strength, for wisdom, and for the ability to rise above my anger and resentment. I asked God to soothe my heart, to help me see Gendry not through the lens of my pain but through the lens of Matthew's needs. I prayed for the patience to speak with respect, even when I didn't feel it, and for the grace to put my son's happiness above my own hurt.

These prayers became a lifeline for me. They reminded me that forgiveness wasn't about excusing Gendry's behavior or pretending that the pain didn't exist. Forgiveness was about freeing myself from the burden of anger and bitterness, about creating space for healing and growth—not just for me, but for Matthew as well. I knew that holding onto resentment would only make co-parenting harder, and I didn't want that for my son.

Building an amicable relationship with Gendry wasn't easy, but it was necessary. I made a conscious decision to focus on what mattered most—Matthew. Every interaction with Gendry, no matter how difficult, was centered around our son. I set boundaries to protect myself emotionally, but I also made an effort to communicate openly and respectfully about parenting decisions. I wanted Matthew to see that, even though his parents were no longer together, they could still work as a team to support him. There were moments when it was incredibly hard. Gendry and I didn't always agree on how to handle certain situations, and there were times when old wounds threatened to resurface. But in those moments, I reminded myself of why I was doing this. It wasn't about Gendry, and it wasn't about me—it was about Matthew. My love for him gave me the strength to keep going, even when it felt impossible.

One of the hardest things to come to terms with was the fact that, no matter how hard I tried, Matthew would inevitably feel the effects of our divorce. I worried about how he would process the absence of a unified family, about whether he would feel like he was missing out on something other children had. I worried that he might blame himself or feel torn between his parents. These thoughts were heartbreaking, and they often left me questioning whether I was doing enough to fill the gaps. But then I reminded myself that while Matthew might miss certain aspects of a traditional family, he would also gain something valuable: the example of a mother who chose happiness, strength, and authenticity. He would see that it's okay to walk away from relationships that aren't healthy, that it's possible to rebuild and thrive after pain, and that love isn't just about staying—it's about choosing what's right for yourself and your children.

The Power of a Happy Parent

I firmly believe that a happy parent creates a happy home. While I couldn't control how Gendry showed up as a father, I could control how I showed up as a mother. I made it my mission to create a home environment that was filled with love, stability, and joy. I wanted Matthew to feel safe, supported, and cherished, even in the midst of such a major transition. I focused on spending quality time with him, creating memories that would remind him of how loved he was. Whether it was reading bedtime stories, playing games, or simply talking about his day, I made an effort to be fully present with him. These moments weren't just for Matthew—they were for me too. They reminded me of why I was fighting so hard to create a better life for both of us.

Over time, I began to find peace in my decision to divorce Gendry and to co-parent with grace. I realized that my marriage ending wasn't a failure—it was a step toward a healthier, happier future. I stopped blaming myself for what went wrong and started focusing on what I could control: the way I showed up for Matthew, the kind of environment I created for him, and the example I set as a mother. I also found peace in my relationship with Gendry. While our marriage hadn't worked out, I could still respect him as Matthew's father. I could still recognize the role he played in our son's life and support their relationship, even if my own connection with him was broken. This mindset allowed me to approach co-parenting with kindness and patience, even on the hardest days.

In the end, I realized that family doesn't have to look a certain way to be meaningful. While Gendry and I were no longer husband and wife, we were still partners in parenting. And while Matthew's family might not look like the traditional ideal, it was still filled with love, care, and dedication. Through prayer, self-reflection, and a commitment to Matthew's well-being, I found the strength to navigate the complexities of divorce and co-parenting. I learned that forgiveness isn't just about letting go of anger—it's about creating space for healing and growth. And most importantly, I learned that my happiness as a mother was the greatest gift I could give to my son.

The Journey to Our Dream Home

There are moments in life that feel like they were divinely orchestrated—moments when everything aligns, and you realize that the dreams you once thought were impossible are not only possible but within reach. For Matthew and me, moving into our dream home was one of those moments. It was a journey filled with challenges, faith, and perseverance, and looking back, I can see how every step led us to where we were meant to be.

The decision for Matthew and me to leave the home Gendry and I had purchased was bittersweet. That house represented a chapter of my life that was filled with both love and pain, but it was time to move forward. Gendry and I had agreed that Matthew would live with me full-time, and while that gave me peace about our next steps, it also came with the responsibility of creating a new home for us—a place where we could start fresh and build a future together. Selling our old home was the first step. I knew it was necessary, but it wasn't easy. Every room held memories of the life we had built as a family, and packing up those memories felt like letting go of a part of myself. But as I boxed up our belongings, I reminded myself that this wasn't the end—it was a new beginning. I was determined to find a home where Matthew and I could thrive, a place where we could create new memories and build the life we deserved.

Years before, when Matthew was around six years old, we had visited a community that left a lasting impression on me. It was a beautiful, prestigious neighborhood with sprawling homes and tree-lined streets. As we drove through, I remember thinking, Wouldn't it be amazing to live here one day? But at the time, it felt like an impossible dream. I wasn't in a financial position to even consider living in a place like that, and the thought of it felt so far out of reach that I quickly dismissed it. But something about that visit stayed with me. It planted a seed of hope, a vision of what could be. Over the years, I kept that dream tucked away in the back of my mind, not knowing if it would ever come true but refusing to let it go completely. I wanted Matthew to have what I never had—a home in a safe, beautiful neighborhood where he could grow up surrounded by opportunities and a sense of stability.

When the time came to search for a new home, I was filled with both excitement and anxiety. I knew what I wanted—a place that felt like a sanctuary for Matthew and me—but finding it proved to be more challenging than I anticipated. Every home we looked at was either out of my budget or didn't feel right. Matthew and I would leave house after house, feeling discouraged, wondering if we would ever find a place that felt like home. But through it all, I held onto my faith. I told Matthew, "Something amazing is coming. We just have to keep believing." Even on the hardest days, when it felt like we were running out of options, I refused to give up. I wanted Matthew to see that faith and perseverance could overcome any obstacle, and I wanted him to know that dreams, no matter how big, are worth pursuing.

As the search dragged on, I decided to take a bold step of faith. I had a basket filled with rocks, each one representing a prayer God had answered in my life. I told Matthew, "Let's put this basket in the back of the truck. Let's pretend that it's going to our new home." I wanted Matthew to see that faith wasn't just about waiting—it was about acting as if the things you believe in are already on their way. That basket became a symbol of hope for us. Every time we looked at it, we reminded ourselves that God had brought us through so much already and that He wasn't finished with us yet. It was a small act, but it kept us focused on the vision of what was to come.

About a week later, everything changed. My realtor sent me an email with a list of new homes, and as I scrolled through the options, one home stood out above the rest. Something about it caught my attention, and I knew I had to see it in person. I called my realtor immediately and scheduled a visit. As Matthew and I drove to the home, I started to recognize the surroundings. My heart began to race as we approached a security gate—the same gate that led to the community I had dreamed of living in all those years ago. I couldn't believe it. Could this really be happening? Could we actually be about to see a home in the very neighborhood I once thought was out of reach?

When we arrived at the gate, a sense of peace washed over me. I knew in my heart that this was it. This was home. As we drove through the neighborhood, everything felt right—the trees, the homes, the atmosphere. By the time we pulled into the driveway, I was certain that this was where we were meant to be.

The house was everything I had hoped for and more. It was beautiful, warm, and inviting—the perfect place for Matthew and me to start our new chapter. I wrote a letter to the owner, pouring out my heart and sharing my vision for making this house our home. Shortly after, my offer was accepted, and on July 21, 2023, Matthew and I moved into our dream home. As we unpacked and settled in, I couldn't help but reflect on how far we had come. What once felt like an impossible dream had become our reality, and it was all because of faith, perseverance, and the willingness to keep believing even when things seemed hopeless. Standing in that home, surrounded by answered prayers, I knew that God's plan for us had been greater than anything I could have imagined.

This journey taught me so much about the power of faith and the importance of never giving up on your dreams. It reminded me that even when the path seems uncertain, even when everything feels like it's going wrong, there is always a way forward. Sometimes, you just have to take that bold step of faith, believing that what you're hoping for is already on its way. For Matthew, this experience was more than just a move—it was a lesson in trusting God, staying hopeful, and working toward something greater. I wanted him to see that dreams aren't just for wishing—they're for pursuing with all your heart. And now, every time we walk through the doors of our beautiful home, I'm reminded of the power of faith and the incredible things that can happen when you trust in something bigger than yourself.

Letting Go of a Life That Was Killing Me

For years, I clung to a life that was killing me—spiritually, emotionally, and mentally. I convinced myself that the life I had built with Gendry was the best I could have, that it was enough. I told myself that my sacrifices were necessary, that staying in a broken marriage was the price I had to pay for stability, for family, for love. But deep down, I knew the truth: I was holding onto something that no longer served me, something that was slowly chipping away at my spirit. When you're in the middle of the storm, it's hard to see beyond the chaos. I thought my life with Gendry was as good as it could get. I couldn't imagine anything better because I had spent so long convincing myself that this was it. But if only I had known what amazing things God had in store for me, I would have let go so much sooner. The life I was holding onto was small compared to the plans God had for me, but at the time, my fear of the unknown kept me from seeing it.

Letting go is one of the hardest things we can do as humans. It requires us to step into uncertainty, to release the safety net we've built for ourselves, and to trust in something greater than what we can see. For me, letting go of my marriage felt like stepping off a cliff. I was terrified of what life would look like without Gendry, of how Matthew would feel growing up in a broken home, of how people would judge me for choosing divorce. The fear was paralyzing, and for a long time, it kept me stuck in a life that wasn't fulfilling. But as much as I feared letting go, I began to realize that staying was no longer an option. Staying in that marriage wasn't just hurting me—it was holding me back from the person I was meant to be. My spirit felt crushed, my emotions were in constant turmoil, and I could feel myself slipping further and further away from the woman I used to be. I knew that if I didn't make a change, I would lose myself completely.

What finally gave me the courage to let go was my faith. I had to believe that God's plan for me was bigger than the life I was holding onto. I had to trust that He had something greater in store, even if I couldn't see it yet. Isaiah 55:8-9 says, "'For My thoughts are not your thoughts, nor are your ways My ways," says the Lord. "For as the heavens are higher than the earth, so are My ways higher than your ways, and My thoughts than your thoughts.'" That verse became a source of comfort for me. It reminded me that I didn't have to understand everything—sometimes, I just had to trust. Letting go wasn't about giving up; it was about surrendering to God's will. It was about believing that He could take the broken pieces of my life and create something beautiful. It was about trusting that His plans were far greater than anything I could imagine. And it was about realizing that my heart, my happiness, and my well-being mattered to Him.

As someone who is deeply against divorce, the decision to end my marriage was one of the hardest I've ever made. I had always believed in the sanctity of marriage, in the idea that love and commitment could conquer anything. I didn't want to break up my home or take away the sense of stability that Matthew deserved. But at the same time, I couldn't ignore the truth: my marriage was no longer a source of love, joy, or partnership. It had become a place of pain, betrayal, and emptiness. Divorce felt like a failure to me, and for a long time, I struggled with guilt. I questioned whether I had done enough, whether I had tried hard enough, whether there was more I could have done to make things work. But as I prayed and reflected, I began to realize that staying in a toxic situation wasn't honoring God—it was dishonoring the woman He created me to be. God's will for my life wasn't for me to live in constant pain; it was for me to live in freedom, joy, and purpose.

One of the most profound lessons I learned during this journey was about my own worth. For years, I had allowed myself to settle for less than I deserved. I had accepted lies, betrayal, and emotional neglect because I didn't fully believe I was worthy of more. I thought that sacrificing my own happiness was the price I had to pay to keep my family together. But through prayer and self-reflection, I began to see myself through God's eyes. Psalm 139:14 says, "I praise You because I am fearfully and wonderfully made; Your works are wonderful, I know that full well." That verse reminded me that I am God's creation, and He doesn't make mistakes. I am worthy of love, respect, and kindness—not because of what I do, but because of who I am.

Sometimes, we hold onto things so small, thinking they are all we'll ever have. We cling to relationships, jobs, and situations that don't serve us because we're afraid to let go. We think, What if this is the best I can do? But what I've learned is that God never calls us to settle. He gives us authority and power to live abundantly, but we can only step into that abundance when we're willing to release what no longer serves us. Letting go of my marriage wasn't just about walking away from Gendry—it was about walking into the life God had prepared for me. It was about trusting that His plans were bigger than my fears. It was about believing that I could have joy, peace, and love again, even after everything I had been through. And it was about choosing to live boldly, knowing that God's promises are always greater than our doubts.

Faith is what carried me through the hardest moments. It reminded me that I wasn't alone, that God was with me every step of the way. When I felt weak, He gave me strength. When I felt lost, He guided me. And when I felt broken, He reminded me that He is a God of restoration. I started to see my life not as a series of mistakes or failures but as a journey of growth and redemption. I realized that every challenge I faced had prepared me for the next step. Every heartbreak had taught me something about myself, and every moment of pain had drawn me closer to God.

As I moved forward, I made a conscious decision to stop living small. God's Word tells us that we have authority over everything, that we are made in His image, and that we are called to live abundantly. So why was I acting like I didn't deserve more? Why was I settling for less than the life God had promised me? Letting go of Gendry was the first step, but it wasn't the last. I began to dream again, to set goals that once felt impossible. I started to see myself not as a victim of my circumstances but as a victor through Christ. And as I stepped into this new chapter, I felt a sense of freedom and joy that I hadn't felt in years.

Looking back now, I can see how everything led me to this moment. God's plan was perfect, even when I couldn't see it. He took what was broken and made it whole. He turned my pain into purpose and my struggles into strength. He reminded me that I am never alone, even in the hardest moments. Letting go wasn't easy, but it was necessary. And in letting go, I found myself, my faith, and the amazing future God had prepared for me.

Choosing to Heal

After the pain and lessons of my marriage and divorce, I made a conscious decision: I would not enter another relationship until I was fully healed. I needed time to reflect, to grow, and to address the parts of myself that had been wounded and neglected. I didn't want to attract the same qualities in a man as I had seen in my father or even in Gendry. I knew that if I didn't take the time to heal, I might continue the cycle, carrying unaddressed pain and attracting relationships that mirrored the past. This was about more than just avoiding toxic relationships—it was about breaking generational curses, breaking barriers both financially and spiritually, and redefining the kind of life and love I wanted for myself and my son, Matthew.

Healing is not an easy process. It requires you to confront parts of yourself that you may have ignored for years. I had to face my fears, my insecurities, and the patterns of behavior that had led me to accept less than I deserved. I had to ask myself hard questions: Why did I stay in situations that hurt me? Why did I feel the need to prove my worth through sacrifice? What beliefs about myself and love had I internalized from my upbringing? One of the most profound realizations I had was that healing wasn't about fixing what was broken—it was about rediscovering what was already whole within me. I wasn't broken. I had been hurt, but my essence, my value, and my spirit were still intact. I just needed to reconnect with them, to nurture them, and to remind myself that I was worthy of love—not just from others, but from myself.

In a world that often equates being single with being incomplete, I made the choice to embrace my singleness. Almost four years after my divorce, I haven't brought any man into my home or introduced anyone to Matthew. It's not because I'm afraid of love—it's because I'm prioritizing the love I have for myself and my son. I've learned that being single isn't a sign of failure or loneliness; it's a testament to strength. It means that I'm capable of standing on my own, of finding joy and fulfillment in my own company. It means that I'm not settling for anything less than what I deserve. It means that I'm taking the time to ensure that when the right person comes into my life, they will add to my happiness, not be the source of it.

For so long, I thought love was about sacrifice—about giving so much of yourself that there was nothing left. But I've come to understand that true love doesn't deplete you; it nourishes you. It's not about losing yourself in another person; it's about two whole people coming together to create something even greater. I want to ensure that the next time I enter a relationship, it's with someone who loves both Matthew and me unconditionally. Someone who doesn't see us as a burden but as a blessing. Someone who respects the life I've built, the boundaries I've set, and the values I hold dear. But before I can expect that from someone else, I have to embody it myself. I have to love myself truly and freely. I have to treat myself with kindness and respect. I have to be the kind of person I want to attract. And I have to trust that when the time is right, God will bring the right person into my life.

This time, I don't want to choose—I want God to choose for me. I've learned that when we try to force things, when we chase after relationships that aren't meant for us, we often end up settling for less than God's best. But when we trust Him, when we surrender our desires and plans to Him, He has a way of bringing us exactly what we need. I believe that the person God has for me will feel like home. It won't be perfect—no relationship is—but it will be right. There will be peace, even in the challenges. There will be love, even in the disagreements. And there will be a sense of alignment, a feeling that this is where I'm meant to be. I also trust that God will reveal the red flags early on. One of the lessons I've learned from my past is that my heart always knows. There were times when I ignored my intuition, when I silenced the voice inside me that was warning me of trouble. But not anymore. I've promised myself that I will listen to my heart and trust the wisdom God has given me.

Right now, my focus is on being the best version of myself and the best mother I can be to Matthew. He is my joy, my inspiration, and my greatest blessing. Every decision I make is with him in mind—what kind of example am I setting? What kind of life am I creating for him? I want Matthew to see that happiness isn't dependent on a relationship. I want him to grow up knowing that his mother is strong, independent, and capable of creating a beautiful life on her own. And I want him to understand that love is about quality, not quantity—that it's better to wait for the right person than to settle for the wrong one.

In choosing to heal, I've also chosen a life of freedom and peace. I'm no longer bound by the expectations of others or the fear of being alone. I'm no longer carrying the weight of past mistakes or the pain of broken relationships. I've let go of what was holding me back, and in doing so, I've created space for something greater. Being single has allowed me to rediscover myself, to pursue my passions, and to build a life that I'm proud of. It's shown me that I am whole, complete, and enough just as I am. And while I'm open to love in the future, I know that my happiness doesn't depend on it. My happiness comes from within, from my relationship with God, and from the love I share with Matthew.

Choosing Faith Over Fear: My Journey to Pursue My Dreams

Have you ever felt a deep pull in your heart—a voice whispering that there's more to life than what you're currently living? That was me, day in and day out, as I sat in my corporate job.

I was working a full-time job during the day and building my business at night. I was always working, constantly exhausted, running on fumes, and questioning if this was the life I was meant to live. Deep down, I knew the answer. There had to be more to all. I was mostly making money for the people who ran my company. I was not doing something that would greatly impact my own life or my own finances. I knew I was capable of so much more, but fear held me back. I asked myself, "What if I leave and fail? What if I can't make it?" These thoughts consumed me. I was stuck in a cycle of hesitation and doubt. But the truth is, my soul knew it was time. It cried out for me to take a leap of faith, to trust that God had something greater waiting for me. I had to step out of my fear and into my purpose.

Fear is a powerful thing. It whispers in your ear, "What if you fail? What if you can't pay your bills? What if you regret this decision?" And for so long, I let those whispers paralyze me. I stayed in a job that drained my energy and spirit because it felt safe. The thought of leaving to pursue my business full-time felt overwhelming. But here's the thing about fear—it only has as much power as you give it.

I started to ask myself a different question: "What if I win? What if stepping into my purpose is the best decision I'll ever make?" I decided to trust God. He was the one who had given me this dream. He would surely have provided me with the tools and expertise needed to fulfill this dream. If God was calling me to work on my business full-time, then this was meant to be. I knew this in the deepest part of my heart. There comes a moment when you can no longer ignore what your soul is telling you. It had been countless days since I was feeling unfulfilled at work. I was miserable, working on autopilot and hoping something would change. I wanted to move forward, but I couldn't. God was calling me to step into something bigger, and while I was scared of the unknown, I was even more scared of staying where I was and missing out on my destiny.

One morning, I woke up with clarity. I called my manager and told him I needed a break—a three-month leave from work to figure things out. Deep down, I knew this wasn't just a break. A few weeks later, I packed up my desk and submitted my resignation letter. I felt a mix of emotions—fear, relief, excitement, and uncertainty. I looked at myself in the mirror that night and said, "God's got you. There is something amazing ahead." Letting go of the familiar was terrifying, but I reminded myself that God's plan is perfect. He is the great "I AM," the one who holds everything in His hands. If He called me to step into this new chapter, then He had already made a way for me to succeed.

Fear is one of the most natural emotions we experience. It's our mind's way of protecting us, of warning us. When you're stepping out of your comfort zone—leaving a job, starting a business, or pursuing a dream—it's completely normal to feel afraid. Fear doesn't mean you're not ready. Fear simply means you're human. The key is not to let fear consume you. It should not decide your choices for you. Fear only has as much power as you give it. You don't have to fight fear; you just have to move forward despite it. That's what it means to be courageous.

I was terrified when I left that job, but I still did it. I was still afraid of failure, but I knew I had to try something new If I wanted to be happy. I asked myself, "What's worse: failing and learning or staying in a place where I know I'm miserable?" The thought of never trying became even more unbearable than the fear of failure.

When you feel fear rising, don't run from it. Instead, acknowledge it:

- "Yes, I'm scared of failing, but what if I succeed?"
- "Yes, I'm uncertain, but I trust that God will guide me."
- "Yes, this is hard, but I'm stronger than I think."

You can be afraid and still trust that God's plans are bigger than your doubts. The Bible reminds us over and over not to be afraid:

- "For God has not given us a spirit of fear, but of power, and of love, and of a sound mind." (2 Timothy 1:7)
- "Do not fear, for I am with you; do not be dismayed, for I am your God." (Isaiah 41:10)

God knows we'll feel fear, but He gives us everything we need to overcome it. Fear may be a part of your story, but it doesn't have to control the narrative. When you place your faith in God, you're reminded that He's in control. Instead of focusing on fear, focus on the promise that lies ahead.

Here are some ways to navigate fear while pursuing your dreams:

1. Pray Through It: Bring your fears to God. Tell Him exactly what you're afraid of and ask for His peace and guidance.

2. Break It Down: Big changes can feel overwhelming. Break your goals into small, manageable steps and tackle them one at a time.

3. Seek Support: Talk to trusted friends, mentors, or family members who can encourage you and remind you of your strength.

4. Visualize Success: Instead of dwelling on what could go wrong, imagine what could go right. See yourself thriving in the life you're working toward.

5. Remind Yourself Why: Write down why you're pursuing this path. When fear creeps in, go back to your "why" and let it reignite your determination.

I think it's perfectly okay to have fear. It's okay to feel uncertain. But don't let it stop you from moving forward. The fact that you're afraid means you're stepping into something bigger than yourself. And that's exactly where growth happens. God doesn't ask us to be fearless; He asks us to trust Him. He asks us to take the next step, even when we don't see the whole staircase. And when you do, you'll realize that fear isn't as powerful as you once thought.

A Youthful Distance

When I entered my early twenties, I drifted away from God. I did not do this on purpose; I was not intentionally thinking that I wanted to move away from God. It just happened. This was not a rejection of him or his power either. Life just got busy. I got distracted, and I could not devote time to prayer, reading the Bible, and connecting with God. The distractions piled on, and I started giving priority to things other than my faith. I knew God existed; I never doubted His miracles or His presence, but I did not nurture or pay attention to faith. I thought I could handle life on my own terms. I did not realize how much I really needed Him.

At that time, I thought that all miracles were grand, extraordinary events—the kind of things you read about in the Bible: the parting of the Red Sea, the feeding of the five thousand, or raising the dead. I never paused to realize the small miracles happening around me every day. Breathing, walking, waking up each morning—these were miracles I took for granted. I didn't see the divine in the ordinary. In my busyness, I missed the beauty of God's creation, of His gift to us—Life.

Since God was no longer anchoring me, I was wandering through life without a purpose. I wasn't miserable, but I wasn't fulfilled either. I was focused on achieving worldly goals—a job, a house, money. I was not tending to my spiritual needs, and this was draining me even though I did not realize it yet. I always felt as if something was missing. I felt empty. I ignored these feelings, thinking I was on the right track. Whenever I felt low, I would make myself busy; I would take on more work, get myself into relationships, and do anything that would make me stop thinking. I was constantly avoiding sitting down alone with my thoughts.

In hindsight, I can see that those moments of emptiness were God calling me back to Him, whispering that the path I was on wasn't enough. But at the time, I wasn't ready to listen. It wasn't until much later that I began to see my life differently. One day, as I watched Matthew play outside, running freely and laughing without a care in the world, it hit me: This is a miracle. His energy, his joy, his life—none of it was guaranteed, but God had given it to me. And then I began to see miracles everywhere. I realized that breathing is a miracle. Our hearts beat without us thinking about it; our lungs fill with air without us asking them to. Each day we wake up is another opportunity, another chance given by God. Even during the times I had turned away from Him, He had been there, guiding me and keeping me going.

I see now that God never left me, even when I left Him. He was there in every struggle, in every moment of doubt, and in every small victory. He was there when I felt lost, silently guiding me toward the life He had planned for me. His grace covered me, even when I didn't see it.

There's one moment that really sticks with me. I remember feeling totally overwhelmed, not having a clue how to move forward. I was just sitting in my room, feeling like everything was unraveling around me. I wasn't praying or anything, but in that quiet moment, I felt this unexpected sense of peace, like someone was wrapping their arms around me and assuring me everything would be alright. I realized that God was reaching out to me, even though I wasn't looking for Him.

As I was becoming a full-fledged adult, I started achieving things I had always been scared about. I had a beautiful home, a reliable car, and a steady income. It looked like I had it all. But there was still a void in me, a feeling that none of it truly mattered. I could have had all the material success in the world, but without God, I would have still felt. There's a verse in the Bible that says, "What does it profit a man to gain the whole world and lose his soul?" (Mark 8:36). That verse began to take on new meaning for me. I realized that no amount of money, success, or comfort could bring me the peace and fulfillment that only God can provide. Life without God wasn't just meaningless—it was unbearable.

It wasn't an overnight transformation, but slowly, I began to turn back to God. I started praying again. Praying was out of obligation, but out of a genuine desire to connect with Him. I began reading my Bible, finding inspiration and solace in its words. The more I leaned into my faith, the more I felt a sense of peace and purpose returning to my life. God became my everything. He became the air I breathed, the song I sang, the foundation of my existence. I no longer saw Him as distant or removed—He was with me in every corner of my life.

As I rebuilt my relationship with God, I knew it was important to pass this lesson on to Matthew. I would often tell him, "No matter where you go in life, keep God close to you." I wanted him to understand that the world can be full of distractions, but nothing was more important than staying connected to God. I tried to show Matthew the importance of faith through my actions, not just my words. I showed him what it meant to live a life centered on faith. We pray together, talk about God's love, and read the Bible. I wanted him to know that God was always with him, no matter what challenges he faced. My greatest hope is that he grows up with a strong foundation of faith, one that will sustain him throughout his life.

Today, I am so grateful for everything that God has done in my life. I'm grateful for the lessons I've learned, the struggles that have shaped me, and the faith that now sustains me. I've learned that life isn't about avoiding pain or seeking perfection—it's about trusting God through every moment. I no longer take the small things for granted. Every breath, every sunrise, every moment with Matthew is a reminder of God's goodness. I see His hand in everything, and I know that as long as I keep Him at the center of my life, I will always have enough.

God is more than just a part of my life—He is my life. He is the reason I wake up each morning with hope. God is the strength that carries me through difficult times, and the joy that fills my heart. I can't imagine life without Him, and I don't want to. He has shown me that His love is constant, unchanging, and always available, no matter how far I may stray.

Nothing in life matters without God. You can have all the success in the world, but without His presence, it will never be enough. My prayer is that others will see this truth and turn to Him, not out of fear or obligation, but out of love and gratitude. To anyone who feels lost or distant from God, I want to say this: He is always there, waiting for you. No matter how far you've gone, no matter how long it's been, His arms are open wide. All you have to do is turn to Him and take care of yourself the same way he cares for you.

Punching Through the Pain:

One of the ways in which I decided to care for myself was by making sure my body was strong, just as my soul was. When I first joined a fitness group just a few minutes from my house, I had no idea how much it would change my life. I wasn't new to working out, but I had never truly experienced the emotional and mental release that came with pushing my body to its limits. I wasn't just there to get stronger physically—I needed something deeper. I needed a way to let go of the emotional weight I had been carrying for years. My favorite class quickly became the 5 AM session. Something about the early morning workouts felt like a reset, a way to start the day with purpose and intensity. But my absolute favorite part of the week was Friday—the day when we boxed. There was something about that class that felt different, almost sacred. It wasn't just exercise; it was therapy.

Each morning, I would drag myself out of bed while the world was still asleep. The streets were dark, the air crisp, and the gym lights shone like a beacon, calling me toward something greater than myself. I would step inside, lace up my gloves, and prepare for whatever the day's workout had in store. There was a rhythm to it—a structure that gave me stability. The warm-up, the circuits, the repetitions. I could lose myself in the movement, let my thoughts quiet, and simply be present. But Fridays were different. Fridays were for boxing, and that was where my true release happened.

The first time I put on the gloves and stood in front of the heavy bag, I didn't think much of it. It was just another workout. But as the class went on, something shifted inside me. With every punch, I felt something stirring deep within me, something I had been suppressing for years. The coach called out instructions, guiding us through combinations, but I barely heard him. My focus was entirely on the bag in front of me. Jab. Cross. Hook. Uppercut. Each punch landed with force, each movement filled with more than just physical effort—it was emotional, raw, unfiltered.

One particular Friday morning, everything came to a head. The moment I started punching the bag, I felt a rush of emotions overwhelming me. At first, I ignored it, pushing through the workout, hitting harder, faster. But then, without warning, the tears came. I was punching, crying, gasping for breath, but I couldn't stop. Each punch was a release—of anger, of pain, of memories I had buried deep within me. I wasn't just punching a bag; I was punching through my past. I was punching for the 15-year-old girl who felt unheard, for the times I had been hurt, betrayed, or doubted. I was punching for every moment I had carried pain in silence.

My coach noticed what was happening but didn't say a word. He didn't try to stop me or tell me to take a break. He knew. He had seen it before—the way physical movement could unlock something deeper. He let me cry, let me keep punching, let me release everything I had been holding in for years. At that moment, I wasn't just a woman in a fitness class. I was someone standing in front of my pain, facing it head-on, refusing to let it control me any longer. And with each hit, I felt lighter.

For years, I had been holding so much inside of me—pain, frustration, disappointment. I had told myself to be strong, to keep moving forward, to push through the pain without truly dealing with it. But the truth is, holding things in doesn't make them disappear. It only makes them heavier. I realized that morning how much I had been carrying. I had smiled through pain, stayed silent when I wanted to scream, and held back tears when I needed to cry. But on that Friday morning, in the middle of that gym, I let it all go. And it felt absolutely amazing.

That day, I learned something powerful: our bodies store pain. When we suppress emotions, they don't just disappear—they live inside us, waiting for a moment to be released. Sometimes, that release comes through tears, through writing, through talking. But for me, that day, it came through boxing. I had spent so much time trying to be strong, trying to move forward without looking back. But healing doesn't happen by ignoring pain—it happens by facing it, feeling it, and letting it go.

After that morning, I never looked at boxing the same way. Every Friday, I approached the bag with a new understanding. It wasn't just about fitness anymore—it was about releasing what no longer served me. Some weeks, it was stress from everyday life. Other times, it was deeper, old wounds resurfacing. But no matter what, I knew that the bag would be there, ready to absorb everything I needed to let go of it all. And the best part? I started to feel lighter in my everyday life. I wasn't just physically stronger—I was emotionally stronger too. I carried myself differently. I spoke with more confidence. I no longer felt burdened by things I hadn't even realized were weighing me down.

Since that day, I've made it my mission to remind others: don't hold it in. When life feels overwhelming, when the weight of the world is pressing down on you, find a way to release it. Scream if you need to. Cry if you have to. Run, box, dance, write—do whatever it takes to get it out. Pain should never stay trapped inside of us. It needs an outlet, a place to go. And when we release it, we create space for something new—peace, clarity, healing.

Now, when I stand in front of the heavy bag, I know that I'm not just training my body—I'm healing my soul. Boxing has become more than just a workout; it's become a way to reconnect with myself, to check in with my emotions, and to remind myself that I am strong in every way that matters. For anyone carrying something heavy, I say this: Don't hold it in. Find your release. Find a way to let it out so you can move forward with lightness, with clarity, with strength. And if that means crying while you punch a bag at 5 AM? So be it. Because sometimes, the best way to heal is to hit back—one punch at a time.

To the Woman Starting Life on Her Own

Stepping into adulthood can feel like standing at the edge of an unfamiliar road. You've finished school, the structure you've relied on is gone, and now you're expected to figure it all out on your own. It's exciting, yes, but also terrifying. You may be asking yourself, "Where do I begin?" or "What if I fail?" Let me tell you this: you are not alone in this journey. Every successful person you admire has stood where you are now—feeling uncertain, overwhelmed, and unsure of what lies ahead. And just like them, you will find your way. God's plan for your life is already in motion, even if you can't see it yet. Take a deep breath. It's okay not to have all the answers right now. You don't need to have it all figured out. You just need to take the first step and trust that God will guide you the rest of the way.

Starting out in life is a process, not a race. It's easy to feel like you're falling behind when you see others landing jobs, buying homes, or building what looks like the "perfect" life on social media. But remember this: everyone's journey is different. What's meant for you will never miss you, and what misses you was never meant for you. Trusting the process means embracing where you are right now. Each step you take—no matter how small—is preparing you for the next season of your life. Growth takes time, and the lessons you learn along the way will shape you into the person you're meant to become. Be patient with yourself. Life isn't about checking off milestones as quickly as possible. It's about becoming who you're meant to be. God's timing is perfect, and He's working behind the scenes, even when you can't see it.

As you begin this new chapter of your life, focus on building a strong foundation. This includes your relationships, your finances, and, most importantly, your faith.

1. Relationships: Surround yourself with people who uplift and support you. Seek out mentors who can guide you, friends who celebrate your wins, and loved ones who pray for your success. Remember, you don't have to do life alone.

2. Finances: Start small, but start now. Create a budget, save even the smallest amounts, and avoid comparing your financial journey to others'. Financial independence begins with discipline, and it will empower you to take control of your life.

3. Faith: Let your relationship with God be the cornerstone of your life. When you lean on Him, you'll find strength in moments of doubt and peace in the midst of uncertainty.

Fear will try to hold you back. It will whisper, "What if you fail?" or "What if you're not good enough?" But here's the truth: fear is a liar.

Faith, on the other hand, is your greatest weapon. When you place your trust in God, you're reminded that you don't have to face life's challenges alone. He is walking with you, guiding your steps, and working all things together for your good.

Whenever fear creeps in, replace it with declarations of faith:

- "God has a plan for my life."
- "I am equipped to handle whatever comes my way."
- "I am not alone; God is with me."

You don't need to have all the answers. You just need to take the next step, trusting that God will light your path. This season of life is about discovering who you are and what you're capable of. It won't always be easy, but every challenge you face is shaping you into the person you're meant to become. Celebrate the small victories: landing your first job, paying your bills, or even just making it through a tough day. These moments are stepping stones toward something greater. And when you experience setbacks, remember that they are not the end of your story. Every failure is an opportunity to learn, grow, and come back stronger. Keep moving forward, and don't be afraid to embrace the journey with all its twists and turns. No matter how tough things get, don't give up. Progress doesn't always look glamorous or fast—it often looks like small, quiet steps in the right direction. But every step forward is a step closer to your dreams. Stay consistent, even when you don't see immediate results. Keep showing up, keep working hard, and keep trusting that God is working behind the scenes.

You must hold on to one truth: you are stronger than you think. You have overcome so much to get to this point, and you have everything you need to keep going. This is only the beginning of your story. The road ahead may feel uncertain, but it is filled with endless possibilities. Your dreams are valid, your efforts are worth it, and your future is brighter than you can imagine.

The Souls in Line

Our story begins not on Earth but in a place beyond human understanding, where eternity stretches endlessly. It is a place of pure light, harmony, and infinite connection—a realm of souls, gathered near the throne of God. These souls exist in perfect communion with one another and with their Creator, filled with an eternal peace that surpasses all comprehension. Yet, even in this divine perfection, there is an opportunity, a gift, that not all souls have experienced: the chance to live a human life on Earth. There is a line in this realm, a line of souls waiting patiently for their turn to descend to Earth. Some souls, radiant and eager, whisper excitedly to one another about the beauty of the human experience. Others, quieter and more contemplative, stand in stillness, preparing for the challenges they know lie ahead. For these souls, going to Earth is a privilege, a sacred contract they make with God, to leave their celestial home and take on the form of a human, with all the emotions, struggles, and triumphs that come with it.

Before each soul descends, they meet with God to understand their purpose. The Creator speaks to them with a voice full of love and wisdom, explaining that life on Earth is a fleeting but extraordinary journey. "You will feel pain," God tells them, "But you will also feel joy. You will know sorrow, but you will also know love. Every emotion, every experience, will shape you, teach you, and bring you closer to understanding the depths of My love." The souls are given no memory of their celestial home once they arrive on Earth, for part of the human experience is to rediscover their connection to the divine. They are told that their time on Earth is temporary, a fleeting moment compared to the eternity of their true existence. "Do not waste it," God says. "Live fully. Feel everything. Learn from every experience, good or bad, and use your life to reflect the glory of My throne." The souls, filled with gratitude and purpose, accept the contract. They descend to Earth, where they forget their divine origin and begin the journey of living as humans.

One day, as I reflected on the complexities of life—the highs and lows, the struggles and triumphs—I heard a story about these souls, waiting in line to experience life on Earth. The story stirred something deep within me, a question I couldn't shake: What if it's true? What if there really are souls waiting for the opportunity to live this life, a life that I sometimes take for granted? The thought changed the way I saw everything. What if every moment—every laugh, every tear, every quiet sunrise and stormy night—was something sacred? What if the pain I had endured, the mistakes I had made, and even the heartbreaks that had broken me were all part of the contract I had made before I came here? If that were true, how could I waste another moment of this life, holding back or letting fear and regret guide me?

With this new perspective, I began to see life differently. I started to appreciate the small things—the way sunlight streamed through the curtains in the morning, the warmth of a cup of coffee in my hands, the sound of Matthew's laughter filling the house. These weren't just ordinary moments; they were treasures, reminders of the beauty of being alive. Even the difficult moments took on a new meaning. The heartbreak I had endured, the betrayals I had suffered, and the challenges that had tested me became part of a larger story—a story of growth, resilience, and discovery. I no longer saw these experiences as things to avoid or escape. Instead, I embraced them as part of the contract I had made when I came to Earth. I began to believe that each experience, no matter how painful, was teaching me something, shaping me into the person I was meant to be.

One of the most profound realizations I had was about the purpose of pain. If the story of the souls was true, then pain wasn't something to fear—it was something to learn from. It was a reminder of what it meant to be human, a chance to grow closer to God by relying on His strength in moments of weakness. I started to see pain not as an obstacle but as an opportunity. It reminded me that I was alive, that I was capable of feeling deeply and fully. It pushed me to look within, to heal old wounds, and to become more compassionate toward myself and others. It taught me that even in the darkest moments, there is light to be found if we have the courage to seek it. As I continued to reflect on the story of the souls, I realized that part of my journey was to help others see the beauty and power of God's throne. I wanted to show people that their lives, no matter how ordinary or challenging they seemed, were extraordinary gifts. I wanted them to know that their struggles had meaning, that their pain was not wasted, and that their joy was a reflection of God's love. I began to share this perspective with those around me, reminding them to live fully and appreciate every moment. "What if this is what you signed up for?" I would ask. "What if your life, with all its ups and downs, is exactly what your soul wanted to experience?" These conversations sparked something in people—a sense of wonder, a new way of seeing their lives, and a reminder of their connection to something greater.

This new way of thinking changed how I approached life. I no longer held back out of fear or doubt. I laughed louder, cried harder, and loved more freely. I let myself feel every emotion without shame or hesitation, knowing that this was part of what it meant to be human. I stopped worrying so much about what others thought of me and started focusing on living a life that felt true to my soul. I also let go of the need to control everything. I trusted that God's plan for my life was greater than anything I could imagine, and I surrendered to His guidance. I believed that as long as I stayed connected to Him, as long as I lived with faith and gratitude, I would fulfill the purpose I had come here for. Thinking about the souls waiting in line to come to Earth filled me with gratitude for the life I had been given. I realized that even the challenges I faced were blessings, opportunities to grow and to experience the depth of what it means to be alive. I no longer saw life as something to endure but as something to celebrate. Every day, I remind myself that this life is a gift, a sacred contract I made with God. I don't want to waste a single moment of it. Whether I'm facing joy or sorrow, success or failure, I choose to embrace it all. Because I know that one day, when my time on Earth is over, I'll return to that realm of light and connection, and I'll be able to say, I lived. I felt. I loved.

The Pain and Beauty of Change

As I've moved through life, I've learned that change is both painful and beautiful. Leaving Haiti was one of the hardest decisions I ever made. It meant leaving behind the only home I had ever known, stepping into an uncertain future, and saying goodbye to people I loved. But it also opened doors to opportunities I never could have imagined. Change also came in the form of personal growth. The person I am today is not the same as the person I was years ago. I've had to let go of old habits, old beliefs, and even old versions of myself to make room for the person I'm becoming. And while that process hasn't always been easy, it's been worth it.

Now, I've created a life that once seemed impossible—a life filled with opportunities, success, and joy. I've worked hard to provide a stable and loving environment for my son, Matthew, making sure that he has the chances I never did. I am now reaping the benefits of everything that I faced and overcame.

Yes, I have faced hardships. But those are the things that have made me who I am today. They have made me stronger and showed me that one failure does not mean the end.

I've learned to see every challenge as an opportunity for growth and every setback as a stepping stone to something greater. I realize how much I've gained from the experiences, good and bad.

While my journey is far from over, I know that I am exactly where I'm meant to be. One of the greatest lessons I've learned is the importance of living with purpose. Life is too short to take for granted, too precious to waste on fear or regret. Every day is an opportunity to grow, to love, and to make a difference in the lives of others. I want to use my story to inspire others, to show them that no matter where they come from or what they've been through, they can create a life filled with meaning and joy.

Today, I carry my past with me—not as a burden but as a source of strength. My roots in Haiti remind me of where I come from, and my journey reminds me of how far I've come. Knowing how far I have come and how I have evolved, I now face my future with hope, faith, and gratitude.

www.ingramcontent.com/pod-product-compliance
Lightning Source LLC
Chambersburg PA
CBHW071529100726
47908CB00004B/1341

* 9 7 9 8 9 9 9 1 0 1 0 1 3 *